FROM ONE JOB
TO THE NEXT

*Worker Adjustment In A
Changing Labor Market*

Adam Seitchik *and* **Jeffrey Zornitsky**

1989

W. E. UPJOHN INSTITUTE for Employment Research

Library of Congress Cataloging-in-Publication Data

Seitchik, Adam.
    From one job to the next : worker adjustment in a changing labor
market / Adam Seitchik, Jeffrey Zornitsky.
       p.   cm.
    Includes bibliographical references.
    ISBN 0-88099-078-3. — ISBN 0-88099-077-5 (pbk.)
    1. Plant shutdowns—Government policy—United States. 2. Manpower
policy—United States. 3. Occupational retraining—Government
policy—United States.   I. Zornitsky, Jeffrey. II. Title.
HD5708.55.U6S45   1989   89-37205
331.12'72'0973—dc20   CIP

∞

THE INSTITUTE, a nonprofit research organization was established on July 1, 1945.
It is an activity of the W. E. Upjohn Unemployment Trustee Corporation, which was
formed in 1932 to administer a fund set aside by the late Dr. W. E. Upjohn for the
purpose of carrying on "research into the causes and effects of unemployment and
measures for the alleviation of unemployment."

THE AUTHORS

Adam Seitchik received his Ph.D. from Boston University. He is assistant professor of economics at Wellesley College and a consulting economist for Abt Associates Inc. He has authored several articles on worker displacement and most recently was a contributor to *Job Displacement: Consequences and Implications for Policy,* edited by John T. Addison.

Jeffrey Zornitsky is director of the Human Resources Consulting Group at Abt Associates Inc. He consults with corporations and government on human resources policy and management, and has published several articles and monographs. He is currently preparing a monograph on corporate strategies for addressing labor shortages. Mr. Zornitsky has an M.A. in economics from Northeastern University.

This monograph was prepared by Abt Associates Inc. under a research grant from the W. E. Upjohn Institute for Employment Research. It does not represent the official opinion or policy of the Institute or Abt Associates. The authors are solely responsible for the contents.

PREFACE

Although the American economy has enjoyed unprecedented growth since the early 1980s, it has substantially accelerated its transition from goods production to service employment. One result of this has been a shift in job opportunities from the hands of American workers to their minds. More than ever before, blue-collar jobs are being replaced by new white-collar opportunities in the professional, sales, and administrative support fields. Employers are also increasingly demanding workers with up-to-date skills who can perform successfully in a more complex and demanding workplace. To succeed in today's labor market, it is clear that workers must be well equipped with relevant and quality education and training.

While these changes may be to the benefit of the American economy, they have also displaced and caused hardship among millions of workers. Blue-collar workers and those from the manufacturing sector have been particularly hard hit as a result of mismatches between the skills they possess and those required in the economy's growing sectors. Even among all displaced workers, the postlayoff readjustment process does not characterize conventional attributes of a flexible labor market. While the American economy may have produced unprecedented growth, many segments of the labor force have been unable to benefit from it.

If these developments were simply the result of recent economic changes, they could be viewed as temporary and requiring short-term adjustment policies. By all accounts, however, they are part of a long-term trend which accelerated in the early 1980s, and which is projected to continue well into the future. Jobs are expected to change even more frequently than in the past; they are also projected to require more complex and higher levels of education and training. At the same time, fewer workers will be available to fill these jobs. Between now and the year 2000, the nation's labor force is expected to grow more slowly and age more rapidly than at any time since the 1930s. These trends will make flexible labor market adjustment even more important than in the past, and particularly among experienced mature workers such as those recently displaced from their jobs. From a policy perspective, this makes it very clear that facilitating the movement of workers from one job to another will continue as a major challenge for the future.

The motivation for this book was supplied not only by the timeliness of the subject, but also by certain observations about the nature of the problem and policies to ameliorate it. After nearly seven years of experience designing policies and operating programs for displaced workers, it has become evident that we have only a limited capacity to help these workers find new jobs that make the most of their skills and accumulated experience. We are, for sure, adept at facilitating reemployment and operating efficient programs, but we are less able to cope with the programming and resource requirements associated with substantive retraining for jobs that offer wages comparable to those earned at the time of layoff.

Resolving this issue is a complex matter that involves several important considerations. Perhaps most fundamental is understanding how changes in the structure of jobs affect the postlayoff adjustment process and policies to facilitate it. Since shifts in the nature of job opportunities largely define both the problem and solution for worker displacement, one cannot help but ask how they might shape worker adjustment patterns as well as the feasibility of alternative policy strategies. Addressing this question is at the heart of effective public employment and training policy and forms much of the basis of this book.

The purpose of this book is to convey to a broad audience an appreciation of how the structure of job opportunities has changed over the past 20 years, and to link these changes to the issues of displacement policy and worker mobility. This is accomplished by examining national and regional data over time and also by analyzing the labor market experience of workers displaced from their jobs between 1981 and 1986. On the basis of the information presented in this book, we hope to contribute to a better understanding of the worker adjustment process and the challenges that future policy will face in addressing it.

In preparing this book, support was forthcoming from several parties. We are grateful to the W. E. Upjohn Institute for Employment Research for providing financial support. We also appreciate the helpful guidance and advice provided by our friends and colleagues. Dr. Louis Jacobson of the Upjohn Institute helped immensely in crafting the analysis plan and commenting on early drafts. Dr. Howard Bloom of New York University and Ms. Jane Kulik of Abt Associates also offered helpful advice on early drafts of the book. Finally, none of this would have been possible without the continued support and encouragement provided by our families and friends.

Jeffrey Zornitsky
Study Director
Abt Associates Inc.

CONTENTS

TABLES

1
Worker Adjustment in Perspective

Those who embrace economic development as a goal must accept change. New products, services, and production processes require the reorganization of capital and labor, the building of new machines, and the learning of new skills. With adaptation to the new, comes elimination of the old; a dynamic economy is by definition one that challenges tradition. Like the village giving way to the city and agriculture to industry, economic development is an evolutionary process which reminds us of Darwinian natural selection.

Despite the similarities between natural and economic evolution, the comparison is as dangerous as it is misleading. The natural world operates through a violent, but elegant, barbarism. Economic development, on the other hand, can be barbaric, but need not be so. At its worst, "progress" destroys communities, leaving workers and their families unemployed without usable skills, and vulnerable to personal and financial loss. At its best, change is (using the economist's term) "Pareto optimal," creating an overall benefit without harming anyone in particular. In the history of our country, it is doubtful that any episode of economic development was Pareto optimal, but this does not alter the fact that growth is a social process subject to our control.

All countries that pursue the goal of economic development and change have institutions to support the flexible allocation of workers and capital. Japan's system of lifetime employment, for example, allows for the retraining and reallocation of workers within the firm (though there is obviously limited interfirm mobility). In Sweden, where layoffs are more common, the state and its labor market boards play an important role in the readjustment process. In the United States, we have developed a system closer to the free market ideal, in which the price of growth is paid in large part by the workers affected by change.

The human cost associated with economic change leads to tension in all economic systems. In the U.S., the latest wave of change has purged hundreds of thousands of workers from their jobs, most in the goods-producing sectors. Many of these job-losers have suffered substantially, experiencing long periods of joblessness and declining real earnings. Understandably, workers remaining in goods-production and other mature industries have sharpened their concerns about job security. The industrial relations system has formed the beginning of a response in the shape of negotiated settlements that better protect workers from layoff. In return, workers have ceded to management demands for wage moderation and more intracompany flexibility.

These changes are slowly moving throughout the economy, representing a free market "contract renegotiation" in response to the risks of economic change. But in the main, the U.S. system continues to rely on the opportunities created through the unrestricted ability of employers to lay off workers, to close plants, and to move capital.[1] For the most part, our society has embraced this flexibility—and the hardship associated with it—as an essential ingredient within a dynamic economy.

The public policy response to displacement pressures in the United States has been tentative and experimental, exerting little fundamental, institutional influence upon the panorama of growth and change. Ironically, the public policies that have most recently affected the level and nature of displacement from manufacturing and other trade-sensitive sectors have done so unintentionally. The deep recession at the beginning of this decade—largely an anti-inflation strategy—brought manufacturing to its knees. Expansionary fiscal policy since that time, in combination with tight money, maintained real interest rates at a high level and drove up the value of the dollar. When combined with tax reform legislation and a doubling of real military spending, these policies resulted in an unprecedented, noninflationary economic expansion. But the strong dollar and high real interest rates also created a favorable climate for the consumption of imports and for foreign investment, while sales by American manufacturers suffered in both domestic and foreign markets.

The macroeconomic policies of the early 1980s were not in and of themselves a fundamental cause of the long-term decline in goods-production. The movement of employment away from manufacturing and into services has been part of a long-term trend. The type and mix of fiscal and monetary policies did, however, work to accelerate the rate of change. What might have been a rising tide of transition became a wave of plant closings and layoffs. According to the Bureau of Labor Statistics, almost 11 million workers were displaced from their jobs because of plant closings or employment cutbacks in the five years leading up to January 1986.[2] Despite the economic expansion, which began in October 1982, the General Accounting Office has estimated that over 16,000 establishments with 50 or more employees either closed altogether or permanently laid off workers during 1983 and 1984 alone.[3]

A unique feature of recent economic change is the effect it has had on the mobility of workers. For the 11 million displaced workers, the road to recovery became blurred by large-scale changes in the composition and hiring requirements of jobs. At the same time that blue-collar jobs were giving way to new, white-collar opportunities, employers were increasingly demanding better educated and trained workers. One result of this was the emergence of (human capital) gaps in the education and hiring requirements of declining and growing jobs. High-wage jobs as well as low-wage jobs were taking on a new character, shifting from goods-production to service industries, and from the "hands" of the workers to their "minds." In this environment, job loss often meant long-term unemployment and earnings loss.

Against this backdrop of change, the federal government instituted new policies and programs to facilitate the transition of workers to new jobs. Whether it be through retraining, remedial education, or simply job search assistance, these policies and programs were intended to help workers find new, meaningful jobs as the economy continued its long-term shift from goods-production to service employment.

The Legislative and Program Framework

In the labor market, the policy approach has been to focus more on ameliorating the effects of change rather than on modifying the process of change itself. Training and education for employed workers are viewed largely as a private responsibility for the employer and employee to negotiate. Despite the increasingly important role of skills-upgrading, the public's strategy is to assist workers only after the process of change has affected them.

The closest the United States has come to an institutionalized policy which facilitates economic change while protecting workers has been the varied set of displaced worker programs in place, on and off, since 1961. The most recent long term program—Employment and Training Assistance for Dislocated Workers—was established under Title III of the Job Training Partnership Act (JPTA) of 1982. This program, recently replaced by the Economic Dislocation Worker Adjustment Assistance Act, was administered by the states, who received an annual, formula-based allocation to assist dislocated workers in obtaining unsubsidized employment. Eligibility for the program was left to the discretion of the states within broadly established guidelines. These guidelines were intended to direct Title III to individuals unlikely to return to their old industries and occupations by focusing on those who:

> (1) have been terminated or laid off or who have received a notice of termination or layoff from employment, are eligible for or have exhausted their entitlement to unemployment compensation, and are unlikely to return to their previous industry or occupation;
> (2) have been terminated, or who have received a notice of termination of employment, as a result of any permanent closure of a plant or facility; or
> (3) are long-term unemployed and have limited opportunities for employment or reemployment in the same or a similar occupation in the area in which such individuals reside, including any older individuals who may have substantial barriers to employment by reason of age.

The implicit goal of Title III was to reemploy as many dislocated workers as feasible in new, expanding occupations and industries, and to do so through retraining and related program services. The legislation provided states with substantial discretion in selecting an appropriate mix of services from among a long list of authorized activities, such as job search assistance, occupation skills training, relocation assistance, and supportive services.

While the intention of Title III was to provide states with the flexibility to develop programs to meet their own unique needs, most adopted a relatively short-term intervention strategy, acting much like a safety net for workers unable to cope successfully with the pace and nature of economic change. During the first three full program years, stretching from July 1984 to June 1987, the states spent roughly $538 million to serve some 386,000 individuals. At an average cost of $1,400 and a 20-week mean duration of participation, Title III did not emerge as a major force in retraining America's unemployed workforce for tomorrow's jobs.

Several factors have contributed to this. For one thing, the absolute level of Title III funding has been sufficient to serve only a small proportion of all potentially eligible dislocated workers. Between 1981 and January 1986, for example, 1.75 million workers 20 to 61 years of age were displaced from full-time private sector jobs annually.[4] Assuming the average cost of $1,400, nearly $2.5 billion would be required to serve these individuals at current investment levels, well above the annual Title III allocation. Even if we grant that 60 percent of these individuals will obtain employment themselves, nearly $1 billion would still be needed to serve just over 700,000 dislocated workers each year. For state and program operators faced with a potential demand for training assistance that well exceeds existing capacity, it is quite natural for them to spread available resources across as many individuals as feasible.

Limited dollars does not imply that increased funding levels will necessarily lead to more costly and lengthy investments. Rather, a natural response to higher funding levels would be to extend services to a larger fraction of the eligible population. Indeed, the experience under Title III suggests that when faced with funding increases, states chose to expand rather than intensify their service strategies. As shown below, program expenditures increased over the first three years of Title III, and so did the number of individuals served; as expected, the mean duration of stay (a reasonable proxy for investment intensity) remained fairly stable.

JTPA Title III Program Expenditures, Service Levels and Duration of Stay, by Year

	PY84	PY85	PY86
Program expenditures (in 000s)	160,332	184,446	193,312
Program participants (in 000s)	178	208	211
Mean weeks of total participation	18	19	20

SOURCE: Job Training Annual Status Report, Employment and Training Administration, U.S. Department of Labor, unpublished data.

Beyond funding levels, the personal costs of program participation also contributed to the short-term program strategy adopted under Title III. To begin, most dislocated workers qualify for unemployment insurance (UI) and a large proportion of them exhaust their benefits within the standard 26-week time frame. Since Title III was not, by design, intended to extend the UI benefit period, and because supportive services (including subsistence payments) were limited to 15 percent of total program expenditures, longer-term program participation was contingent upon workers finding alternative sources of income, such as night jobs, the earnings of other family members, and savings. For that matter, the very participation in JTPA can be a costly endeavor since unemployed dislocated workers need a job as much as they may need some measure of retraining.

As a result, unless they offered the promise of immediate reemployment, programs experienced substantial difficulty attracting dislocated workers. Available evidence indicates that dislocated workers are reluctant to enroll in employment and training programs partly because of their focus on rapid reemployment.[5] According to a recent GAO study, for example, only 26 percent of Title III participants received classroom skills training, while 66 percent received job search assistance.[6] Moreover, of those who did receive training, their median duration of program participation was only nine weeks.

No doubt, even these modest investments have alleviated some of the private and possibly social costs of displacement. Placement rates under Title III have been high—70 percent during the 12-month program year ending in June 1987—and workers have been able to average $6.33 an hour on their new jobs.[7] Whether the program's investments have helped dislocated workers achieve employment and earnings levels above what would have otherwise occurred, however, is another issue. So too is the issue of earnings loss. While Title III programs may be able to affect earnings favorably, it is still quite plausible for workers to experience significant declines relative to the layoff job.

Indeed, this mixed result has emerged in several studies of the effectiveness of employment and training programs for displaced workers.[8] Despite evidence showing favorable earnings impacts, displaced workers still earned less than they did on their layoff job. In one study of several demonstration projects established by the state of Texas, for example, workers experienced an average earnings loss of approximately 33 percent, despite the presence of earnings gains.[9] This result is not qualitatively different from the national experience of dislocated workers and highlights the reemployment focus of the JTPA program.

The result also points up how recent shifts in the structure of job opportunities have frustrated the efforts of employment and training programs to facilitate worker adjustment to economic change. The primary issue here has to do with occupational and industry job-changing.

As commonly defined, displaced workers are individuals who have lost their jobs through no fault of their own and who are unlikely to return to their old industries and occupations. Several studies have shown that about half of displaced workers obtaining reemployment actually return to their same broad industry and occupational groups, however.[10] Largely as a result of emerging human capital gaps, those who do change industries and occupations are found to be most likely to experience an earnings loss. Absent retraining and education services that enable workers to obtain comparable-wage jobs, the implicit goal of Title III to move workers to new, growing sectors may well come in conflict with a worker's primary objective of limiting earnings loss.

This conflict is at the heart of developing effective employment and training programs for dislocated workers. While JTPA is focused on the goal of reemployment, per se, it is difficult to divorce it totally from the issue of earnings loss. Changes in the structure of job opportunities, together with worker interest in minimizing earnings loss, leave reemployment as a necessary but often insufficient condition for program success. The key issue faced by policymakers is determining how to design policies and programs that fit with both worker interests and needs and the structure of changing opportunity.

Emerging Policy Issues

In the summer of 1988, the Congress enacted new trade legislation designed to strengthen employment and training for displaced workers. Among the provisions of this legislation is a new program for displaced workers that replaces Title III of JTPA. The new program—the Economic Dislocation and Worker Adjustment Assistance Act (EDWAA)—requires that 80 percent of the funds available be allotted, by formula, to the states. The remaining 20 percent can be reserved by the Secretary of Labor for discretionary purposes.

Of the funds received by the states, up to 40 percent may be set aside by the governor for administration, technical assistance, and coordination, as well as to support statewide, regional, or industrywide projects, including rapid-response activities to address unexpected plant closings and mass layoffs. The remaining 60 percent is allocated to local Service Delivery Areas with a population of at least 200,000, according to a formula prescribed by the governor.

With the exception of selected other changes in the governance structure of JTPA, the EDWAA program will closely resemble Title III of JTPA. While EDWAA does authorize the establishment of a voucher system, it continues to provide states, and now SDAs, with substantial discretion in selecting programs and services to offer displaced workers. Skills training, job search assistance, support services, and relocation remain among the services authorized under the program. EDWAA does, however, increase JTPA's current 15 percent spending limitation on support services to 25 percent, reflecting the importance of such services to successful program participation.

In many respects, the EDWAA program represents a new set of challenges. After nearly six years of experience under Title III, the expectation is that EDWAA will strengthen the nation's response to economic dislocation and worker adjustment. But such improvements may be evasive. Despite the experience and knowledge gained under Title III, critical issues still remain to be resolved.

Perhaps most important is achieving a better understanding of the feasibility of facilitating worker adjustment. This has proved to be a more complex undertaking than initially envisioned, largely because of the experienced nature of dislocated workers and the pace and nature of structural changes in the economy. As such, it is important to place the issue of worker adjustment in the context of the changing structure of job opportunities in the U.S. These changes have reshaped many of the mobility avenues available to workers and have also limited their ability to obtain new jobs that offer wages commensurate with their skills and experience.

There are several aspects of the mobility process that have an important bearing on the shape and nature of worker adjustment. Among these are the feasibility of moving from declining to growing sectors and the implications of such moves for earnings; the type and level of training required to facilitate such moves; and the role of short-term training in facilitating mobility while minimizing earning loss.

At the same time, however, it may not always be appropriate to focus solely on the employment and earnings of the dislocated worker. The loss of one's job will likely influence the labor force participation of family members, which, especially in instances of sharp earnings loss, can have a favorable influence on overall family income. It is thus useful and appropriate to also consider the additional earnings that could be generated by a working spouse when considering appropriate worker adjustment policies.

Organization of the Monograph

This monograph is intended to contribute to the formulation of policies and programs designed to facilitate worker adjustment to economic change. We take as our starting point changes in the structure of job opportunities in the U.S. and seek to assess their effect on the post-layoff adjustment process of displaced workers and policies to facilitate it.

Chapter 2 of the monograph focuses on how the structure of job opportunities in the U.S. has changed in the recent past, and those issues and problems the changes may pose for successful worker adjustment. To conduct the analysis, we relied on a uniform series of the March Work Experience Supplements to the Current Population Survey (CPS). The CPS is a monthly survey of a random sample of approximately 60,000 households designed to capture basic information on employment and unemployment in the U.S. In March of each year, a special work experience supplement is administered to obtain more detailed data on the employment and earnings experiences of the American population. Relative to other data sources, the CPS offers two key advantages. First, its size and scope permit detailed analysis for the total population as well as subgroups of it. Second, the annual administration of the March Supplement provides a basis for conducting cross-sectional and time series analysis of labor market trends and developments. The chief drawback of the CPS, however, is the absence of longitudinal information on sample members.

The data used in chapter 2 were obtained from a uniform series of the March Supplements created under the direction of Professors Robert Mare and Christopher Winship. Since the scope of the CPS, as well as key definitional terms and questions, have changed over time, the Mare-Winship data offer a uniform and consistent series of information over time. The data included in this analysis focus on wage and salary workers aged 16 to 61 employed in private, nonagricultural jobs between 1970 and 1985.

Chapter 3 assesses the manner in which displaced workers have responded to changes in the structure of jobs, and the implications that emerge for program policy. Here, we rely on data obtained from the January 1986 Dislocated Worker Supplement to the CPS. These supplemental data were gathered on all household members included in the monthly CPS 20-years-old and over who left or lost a job in the preceding five years because of a plant closing, a permanent reduction in force, layoff without recall, or some similar reason. Those identified as displaced were asked a series of questions relating to both their layoff jobs and their post-layoff employment and earnings experience. All private, nonagricultural wage and salary workers between the ages of 20 and 61 were selected for the analysis.

Like the March CPS, the January Supplement contains a nationally representative sample sufficient in size to conduct subgroup analysis. The January Supplement is also the only available source of data that explicitly identifies displaced workers and reports on selected aspects of their employment and earnings experience. The chief disadvantage of this data set is the lack of longitudinal information on sample members.

The final chapter draws together the conclusions from our analyses for the purpose of identifying the major challenges faced by programs and policies designed to facilitate worker adjustment to economic change. It discusses realistic policy goals and their implications for program strategy.

NOTES

1. On August 4, 1988, the Congress enacted new legislation, the Worker Adjustment and Retraining Notification (WARN) Act, requiring that, under certain conditions, employers with 100 or more employees provide advance notice prior to closing a plant or instituting a mass layoff.

2. Francis W. Horvath, "The Pulse of Economic Change: Displaced Workers of 1981–85," *Monthly Labor Review* (June, 1987).

3. *Dislocated Workers: Extent of Business Closures, Layoffs, and the Public and Private Response,* General Accounting Office, Human Resources Division, Report HRD-86-116BR, July 1986.

4. Between 1981 and January 1986, 8.75 million workers, aged 16 to 61, were permanently displaced from jobs, yielding an annual average of 1.75 million. See chapter 3 for details on the characteristics of these workers.

5. See, for example, Lee Bruno, *Study of Selected Aspects of Dislocated Worker Programs: Final Report,* Employment and Training Administration, U.S. Department of Labor, April 1986.

6. *Dislocated Workers: Local Programs and Outcomes Under the Job Training Partnership Act,* General Accounting Office, Report HRD-87-41, March 1987.

7. Job Training Annual Status Report, Employment and Training Administration, U.S. Department of Labor, unpublished data.

8. See, for example: Howard S. Bloom, *Retraining Delaware's Dislocated Workers: Final Impact Evaluation.* Bloom Associates, Inc., Newton, MA, June 1984. Howard S. Bloom, et al., *Evaluation of the Worker Adjustment Demonstration: Final Report,* Abt Associates Inc., Cambridge, MA, July 1986. Walter Corson, et al., *An Impact Evaluation of the Buffalo Dislocated Worker Demonstration Program.* Mathematica Policy Research, Inc., Princeton, NJ, March 1985. Jane Kulik, et al., *The Downriver Community Conference Economic Readjustment Program: Final Evaluation Report.* Abt Associates Inc., Cambridge, MA, May 1984.

9. Bloom, et al., *Evaluation of Worker Adjustment.*

10. Horvath, "Pulse of Economic Change."

2
Challenges of a
Changing Labor Market

Over the 16 years ending in 1986, the American economy has produced unprecedented job growth and opportunities for its citizens. Employment among American civilians expanded by over 33 million jobs, accommodating the rapid growth of women in the labor force and the aspirations of millions in the baby-boom generation. Between 1970 and 1986, employment growth averaged 2.6 percent per year, representing an overall growth rate for the period of 43 percent, far in excess of the 31 percent experienced during the previous 16 years. And since the depths of the 1980–1982 recession, the economy has managed to produce an unparalleled period of economic recovery. By June 1988, nonagricultural employment was nearly 102 million, higher than at any point in the postwar period. Indeed, there is reason to be impressed with the American economy and its ability to generate jobs.

Despite record levels of economic expansion, the recent growth of job opportunities is not as favorable as it would seem. For one thing, the unemployment rate has shown signs of a strong upward secular trend that only recently began to fall to levels comparable to the late 1970s. In 1979, for example, the nation's unemployment rate stood at 5.8 percent; it peaked at 9.7 percent in 1982, hovered in the 7 percent range for the next four years, and began to drop into the 6 percent range in 1987. It was not until the fourth quarter of 1987 that the unemployment rate dropped back to its 1979 level. And even though the rate fell further to 5.5 percent by the second quarter of 1988, it was still higher than in any year between 1948 and 1973. While the economy may well have produced unprecedented numbers of jobs in recent

13

Table 2.1
Percent Distribution of Unemployment by Reason and Duration

	1970	1974	1979	1986	1987	QII, 1988
Duration of Unemployment						
0–5 weeks	52.3	50.5	48.1	41.9	43.9	46.6
5–14 weeks	31.5	31.0	31.7	31.0	29.5	30.0
15–26 weeks	10.4	11.1	11.5	12.7	12.6	11.2
27 or more weeks	5.8	7.4	8.7	14.4	13.9	12.2
Mean duration (in weeks)	8.6	9.8	10.8	15.0	14.5	13.4
Reasons for Unemployment						
Job-losers	44.3	43.5	42.9	48.9	47.9	46.4
Job-leavers	13.4	14.9	14.3	12.3	13.1	14.4
Reentrants	30.0	28.4	29.4	26.2	26.7	26.7
New entrants	12.3	13.2	13.4	12.5	12.5	12.6

SOURCE: *Handbook of Labor Statistics* and *Employment and Earnings,* Bureau of Labor Statistics, U.S. Department of Labor.

years, it has also generated increasingly higher levels of unemployment for its workers.

The recent decline in the level of unemployment also masks important changes in the composition of unemployment. First, most of the rise in unemployment since the late 1970s can be traced to increases in the duration of joblessness and the number of job-losers (table 2.1). Throughout the 1970s, job-losers represented roughly 43 percent of the unemployed. In 1987, five years after the recession, job-losers represented nearly 49 percent of the unemployed; and even into the second quarter of 1988, the proportion of job-losers was still well above the 1979 average, despite a sharp decline in the nation's unemployment rate.

A similar pattern is evident from the data on unemployment durations. Between 1970 and 1979, the duration of unemployment increased by 25.6 percent. Over the next eight years, there was a 28.7 percent increase in the weekly duration of unemployment, a jump from 10.8 weeks to 13.9 weeks. To put this in another light, nearly 14 percent of the unemployed reported being jobless for at least 27 weeks in 1987. This compares to 8.7 percent in 1979, 7.4 percent in 1974, and 5.8 percent in 1970.

One could argue that the increasing duration of unemployment is voluntary, in the sense that every unemployed individual could surely find a job if he or she really wanted to. It is plausible that rising unemployment is due to jobless workers, and especially those losing relatively high-wage jobs, choosing to wait for another good job rather than take a lower-wage one. While there is certainly a voluntary component to all unemployment, it is hard to imagine that most jobless individuals prefer not working to working. This is particularly the case when one considers those individuals who have contributed most to the recent rise in and increasing duration of unemployment.

Between 1979 and 1986, for example, the number of unemployed persons in the United States increased by nearly 700,000. Of this total increase, 77 percent were married men from intact families. The unemployment rate among married men with a spouse present rose by 57 percent between 1979 and 1986, or from 2.8 percent to 4.4 percent; and even in the second quarter of 1987, the unemployment rate of these individuals stood at 4 percent, higher than at any point throughout the entire decade of the 1970s. Moreover, during the same period, married men accounted for about 36 percent of the total increase in long-term unemployment and experienced a 46 percent rise in their average weekly duration of joblessness. It is difficult to believe that most of these unemployed workers were in a position to wait very long for so-called good jobs.

A more plausible explanation for rising and protracted unemployment is that it reflects unprecedented shifts in the occupational and wage composition of employment opportunities. While changes in the structure of job opportunities are not new to the American economy, two factors distinguish the post-1979 period. The first is the deep and lasting changes brought on by the 1980–1982 recessions (table 2.2). Between 1979 and 1985, the sectoral employment shifts were so large that they nearly equaled and in some cases surpassed those experienced over the entire decade of the 1970s. The result was that millions of American workers, who had been holding their own in goods-producing and semiskilled jobs, were put out of work at record levels. To a large extent, they found themselves faced with reemployment opportunities that were increasingly part time and concentrated in services, occupations requiring advanced education and training, and different regions of the country. To the extent that any of these workers were holding high-wage jobs, their problems

Table 2.2
Recent Changes in the Composition of Employment

	1970	1974	1979	1985	1979–1985 percentage change	1979–1985 absolute change relative to 1970–1979 absolute change
I. Private Nonagricultural Employment (in 000s)[a]						
Goods-Producing						
Industries	23,578	24,794	26,461	24,681	−6.7	61.7
-Manufacturing	19,367	20,077	21,040	19,314	−8.2	100.3
Service-Producing						
Industries	34,749	39,301	47,416	58,220	+22.8	85.3
II. Work Experience of Private Wage and Salary Workers						
16–61 (in 000s)[b]						
Employment in semi-	17,387	18,409	18,501	17,135	−7.4	122.6
skilled positions[c]	(27.5)[d]	(26.8)	(24.3)	(19.6)		
Employment in execu-	8,900	10,247	12,085	16,908	+39.9	151.4
tive, managerial, and	(14.2)	(14.9)	(15.9)	(19.2)		
professional specialty						
positions						
Full year, part-time	3,416	4,500	5,009	6,705	+33.9	106.5
	(5.3)	(6.3)	(6.4)	(7.4)		
Percent share of employ-						
ment in East North						
Central States[e]	22.0	21.0	20.1	18.3	−8.9	94.7

a. Data cover private nonagricultural establishment employment. Obtained from *Employment and Earnings,* Bureau of Labor Statistics, U.S. Department of Labor, January 1987, Table B-1.
b. Data cover work experience of nonagricultural, private wage and salary employees. Calculations based on March Supplement to the Current Population Survey.
c. Semiskilled occupations include operatives, assemblers, transportation handlers, and laborers.
d. Refers to percent of total employment.
e. The East North Central states include Illinois, Indiana, Ohio, Michigan, and Wisconsin.

were compounded by significant shifts in the composition of such jobs (table 2.3).

During the 1970s, for example, jobs in the highest quartile of the full-time wage and salary distribution increasingly emphasized more education and training.[1] What was a gradual shift, however, quickly became a substantial change. Between 1979 and 1985, goods-producing industries lost nearly 16 percent of their high-wage jobs, with all of the gain occurring in the service sector. Similarly, the East North Central states, which held roughly a quarter of all high-wage employment throughout the seventies, experienced a 19 percent decline in

Table 2.3
Changing Composition of High-Wage Employment[a]

	Shares of Wage and Salary Employment				1979–1985 percentage change
	1970	1974	1979	1985	
Education					
Less than 12 years	20.3	17.1	13.3	6.7	−49.6
College degree or more	23.3	25.0	27.5	40.1	+45.8
Occupation					
Executive, managerial, and professional specialty	34.2	32.9	31.7	41.3	+30.3
Semiskilled[b]	16.8	18.8	20.5	13.4	−34.6
Industry					
Private goods-producing industries	53.5	52.4	53.9	45.4	−15.8
Private services-producing industries	46.5	47.6	46.1	54.6	+18.4
Region					
East North Central States	25.7	25.4	24.0	19.5	−18.8
South Atlantic States	11.6	11.5	11.8	13.9	+17.8
New England States	6.3	5.8	5.6	6.6	+17.9
Age-Sex					
Prime-age men	81.6	79.5	76.3	73.3	−3.9
Prime-age women	3.7	4.8	7.1	13.6	+91.6

a. Data refer to workers, aged 16 to 61, employed in the top quartile of the full-time, private, nonagricultural wage and salary distribution. Calculations by authors based on the March Supplements to the Current Population Survey.

b. Semiskilled jobs include operatives, assemblers, transportation handlers, and laborers.

their number of such jobs. And perhaps most important for the workers were the human capital shifts. In 1979, 13.3 percent of all high-wage jobs were held by those with less than a high school diploma and 20.5 percent by semiskilled workers. By 1985, these shares dropped to 6.7 percent and 13.4 percent, respectively. Over 40 percent of high-wage jobs were now held by those with at least a college education and the skills needed to obtain a variety of professional and executive positions. Large proportions of newly unemployed high-wage workers were simply not prepared to compete for these jobs.[2]

The second notable feature distinguishing the post-1979 period is the substantial and adverse effect of changes in the structure of job opportunities on many visible segments of the population with traditionally strong attachments to the labor force. Prime-age men, semiskilled workers, those with limited education, and those residing in the midwest region of the country were disproportionately affected by the shifting pattern of employment growth and decline. Their strong attachment to the labor force and stable employment patterns made these workers prime targets for the adjustment problems caused by swift changes in the structure of job opportunities.

This is reflected in the representation of each group among the long-term unemployed and in the lowest quartile of the full-time wage and salary distribution (table 2.4). While each group experienced a modest reduction in its employment and earnings status during the seventies, the status of each group declined after that so precipitously that prime-age men, for example, witnessed a 32 percent increase in their share of low-wage employment and a 48 percent rise in long-term unemployment. While we can say that these workers were losing ground for several years, their rate of decline since 1979 had not been seen before.

What begins to emerge from this is a pattern of employment growth and decline that suggests a strong link between rising and protracted unemployment on the one hand, and growing mismatches on the other. Many of the workers most affected by the last recession do not appear to have the skills needed to obtain growing jobs. Neither do they seem to have a very strong likelihood of reemployment in the sectors from which they were laid off. In many respects, they are stuck—and unable to find jobs that offer wages comparable to those of the layoff job. While comparable-wage jobs do exist, many of the unemployed tend not to be qualified for some, and unable to obtain others due to a shrinking number of opportunities. For many, the outcome is lengthy unemployment and declining earnings.

It is no wonder, then, that public policy attention has recently turned to the question of a vanishing middle class. Since 1979, an unprecedented number of adult workers with traditionally strong attachments to the labor force have become unemployed. Unlike earlier periods, their unemployment is long term in nature and often results in declining earnings. At the center of this seem to be large structural changes in the composition of employment, changes which

Table 2.4
Changes in the Long-Term Unemployment and Earnings Status of Full-Time Wage and Salary Workers[a]

	Year				1970–1985 percentage change
	1970	1974	1979	1985	
All Full-Time Wage and Salary Workers					
Percent long-term unemployed[b]	12.9	13.7	14.1	20.4	+44.7
Percent employed in lowest earnings quartile[c]	25.0	25.0	25.0	25.0	0.0
Prime-Age Men					
Percent long-term unemployed	11.1	16.1	16.5	24.4	+47.9
Percent employed in lowest earnings quartile	6.7	7.4	9.1	12.0	+31.9
Less than 12 Years Education					
Percent long-term unemployed	14.7	15.4	17.3	23.7	+36.9
Percent employed in lowest earnings quartile	31.8	34.8	37.5	43.1	+14.9
Semiskilled Workers[d]					
Percent long-term unemployed	13.6	12.7	14.0	21.4	+52.9
Percent employed in lowest earnings quartile	30.2	30.7	29.8	32.6	+9.4
Workers in East North Central States					
Percent long-term unemployed	12.1	14.7	14.1	23.5	+66.7
Percent employed in lowest earnings quartile	20.7	21.0	21.4	21.8	+1.9

a. Data refer to wage and salary workers, aged 16 to 61, employed in private, nonagricultural jobs. Estimates calculated by authors based on March Supplements to the Current Population Survey.

b. Refers to workers unemployed for at least 27 weeks.

c. Includes workers in the lowest quartile of the full-time, private, nonagricultural wage and salary distribution.

d. Semiskilled jobs include operatives, assemblers, transporation handlers, and laborers.

began over 15 years ago but were significantly accelerated by the 1980–1982 recessions. The U.S. economy may well have generated record levels of employment opportunities since that time, but several segments of its labor force have been unable to take advantage of them.

Understanding how to improve the labor market's adjustment process is key to present and future employment policy. The magnitude and nature of recent economic events suggest that potentially significant investments in workers may be needed to facilitate their adjustment to change. But, what form should such investments take? Should they be directed toward growing or declining sectors of the economy? And how much retraining will be required to limit individual earnings losses? These questions are at the center of current policy and require careful consideration. The current program landscape developed under Title III of JTPA is characterized by short-term training services, limited financial support, and an overriding concern with placing workers in jobs as quickly as possible. This may well be the most practical strategy to follow, but it will not necessarily lead to the most desirable social or personal outcome. To determine what is an appropriate and feasible strategy to follow requires a closer examination of how job opportunities have changed and how workers have reacted to the change.

In the remainder of this chapter, we examine the changing nature of job opportunities in the United States between 1970 and 1985. Our objective is to assess three types of changes that have a direct bearing on both worker adjustment and policies to facilitate it. These include shifts in the human capital attributes, wage distribution, and geographic location of jobs. The data we rely upon are taken primarily from a uniform series of March Supplements to the Current Population Survey and presented for private, nonagricultural wage and salary workers between the ages of 16 and 61.

Occupational and Educational Upgrading

The growing use of better educated and trained workers has been a characteristic of the U.S. economy since the end of the Second World War. Even since 1970, substantial improvements have been made to the nation's stock of human capital. Taking education as one measure of improvement in human capital, available data show, for example, that the fraction of college graduates in the labor force doubled be-

Table 2.5
Occupational Distribution of Employment Among
Private, Nonagricultural Workers[a]

	1970	1974	1979	1985
Professional	16.4	17.1	18.4	22.4
Sales	11.4	11.3	11.5	13.9
Admin. support	16.6	16.4	17.1	16.2
Service	14.6	14.5	14.8	14.6
Crafts	13.4	13.9	13.9	13.4
Semiskilled	27.7	26.8	24.4	19.5

a. Data cover private, nonagricultural wage and salary workers aged 16 to 61. Calculations by authors based on March Supplements to the Current Population Survey.

tween 1970 and 1985. Reflecting improvements in the educational preparation of the labor force, there has also been a clear and steady shift away from semiskilled employment and toward greater use of white-collar professional workers. In 1985, professional workers accounted for 22.4 percent of total employment among private, nonagricultural wage and salary workers (table 2.5). This compares to a share of 16.4 percent in 1970, and a 30 percent decline in the share of employment attributable to semiskilled workers.

The shift toward better educated and trained workers has not been confined to certain industry sectors. Occupational and educational upgrading have been experienced by all sectors of the economy. Goods-producing and service industries alike have significantly increased their use of highly educated and trained labor (table 2.6). The goods-producing sector also increased its use of high school graduates, but like the service sector, cut substantially its reliance on semiskilled workers. In the goods sector, the share of semiskilled jobs declined from 49 percent in 1970 to 37 percent in 1985; similarly, this occupational group dropped from 13.4 percent of service sector employment to 11 percent.

Over time, steady but gradual shifts toward greater use of better educated and trained workers benefit the economy and provide the flexibility workers need to adapt to changes in labor demand. If, as has been the case since 1979, these shifts are accelerated and substantial, they can cause a glut of unemployed workers who are unqualified for new, growing jobs and unable to readily obtain reemployment. The

Table 2.6
Education and Occupational Composition of Goods- and Service-Producing Industries[a]

	U.S. 1985	Goods-Producing Industries				Service-Producing Industries			
		1970	1974	1979	1985	1970	1974	1979	1985
Education									
Less than high school	19.1	40.7	34.9	29.3	22.7	31.9	26.4	22.4	16.5
High school graduate	42.2	40.2	42.2	45.3	45.8	41.0	41.8	41.4	40.7
Some college	20.9	11.8	13.8	15.4	17.1	16.9	18.8	21.3	23.1
College graduate	17.7	7.3	9.0	10.0	14.4	10.1	13.0	14.9	19.7
Occupation									
Professional	22.4	12.9	12.9	13.6	18.9	18.7	19.7	21.3	24.0
Sales	13.9	2.3	2.1	2.5	2.9	17.6	17.2	16.8	19.3
Admin. support	16.2	11.5	10.7	11.6	11.1	20.1	20.1	20.4	18.6
Service	14.6	2.0	1.9	1.6	1.9	23.0	22.5	22.5	20.8
Crafts	13.4	22.6	24.5	24.9	28.2	7.2	7.2	7.5	6.4
Semiskilled	19.5	48.7	47.9	45.8	37.3	13.4	13.2	11.5	10.9

a. Data cover private, nonagricultural wage and salary workers aged 16 to 61. Calculations by authors based on March Supplements to the Current Population Survey.

Table 2.7
Occupational Shares of Net New Employment[a]

	1970–1974	1974–1979	1979–1985
Professional	24.6	31.2	47.5
Sales	10.4	12.8	29.8
Administrative	14.7	23.5	10.3
Service	13.4	17.2	13.5
Crafts	19.9	13.8	10.4
Semiskilled	17.0	1.5	−11.5

a. Data cover private, nonagricultural wage and salary workers aged 16 to 61. Calculations by authors based on March Supplements to the Current Population Survey.

recent record of employment growth and decline suggests that this has been the case. Since 1979, a sharp divergence has developed between the human capital attributes of growing and declining jobs, contributing to longer spells of unemployment and a deterioration in the labor market standing of experienced semiskilled workers. In some cases, the human capital differences are sufficiently large to question the feasibility of worker displacement policy that is targeted on growth sectors of the economy.

To provide some perspective on the issue, consider first the recent contribution of professional and sales jobs to total employment growth (table 2.7). Between 1979 and 1985, almost half of all new jobs created by the economy were professional, and an additional 30 percent were in the sales field. These rates of contribution to employment growth were at least double those of earlier periods, and far greater than those of blue-collar jobs.

Just as these occupations were increasing their share of total employment, they were also making more use of college educated labor (table 2.8).[3] In fact, there were large increases in the share of college graduates in all occupational categories. Professional workers, however, led the way, with over 50 percent having at least a college diploma in 1985, compared to 40.5 percent in 1979 and 35.1 percent in 1970. While only 20 percent of sales jobs employed college graduates in 1985, this was nearly double the share in 1970. Moreover, only 13 percent of sales workers do not have a high school diploma, down from 25.5 percent in 1970 and well below the 1985 national average of 19.1 percent.

Table 2.8
Percent Share of Occupational Employment by Selected
Educational Levels[a]

	1970		1979		1985	
	Less than high school	College degree or higher	Less than high school	College degree or higher	Less than high school	College degree or higher
All Workers	35.9	8.8	25.5	12.9	19.1	17.7
Occupational Group						
Professional	9.2	35.1	6.8	40.5	3.2	50.5
Sales	25.5	11.6	21.0	13.8	13.4	20.3
Administrative	15.2	5.3	11.9	7.6	7.2	11.6
Service (incl. personal and household services)	56.4	1.7	48.5	3.3	34.6	4.4
Crafts	42.3	1.8	33.5	3.4	22.8	5.4
Semiskilled	53.6	1.5	57.4	2.3	34.3	2.9

a. Data cover private, nonagricultural wage and salary workers aged 16 to 61. Calculations by authors based on March Supplements to the Current Population Survey.

In contrast to the strong growth of professional and sales occupations, blue-collar jobs and especially semiskilled jobs contributed negatively to employment growth between 1979 and 1985. As discussed earlier, the absolute decline in employment among semiskilled workers between 1979 and 1985 exceeded the total level of employment growth for the group in the previous nine-year period. Since relatively few semiskilled workers had completed college or professional training, unemployment presented the difficult task of finding new job opportunities in a labor market using more high-level human resources than at any time in the past 16 years.

Over the same period, however, the economy also generated jobs that require limited skills and training. In the growing service-producing sector, for example, nearly 40 percent of all jobs remain in clerical and service occupations, despite this sector's equally heavy reliance on high-level human resources. And even though service occupations increased their share of college graduates, 34 percent of service workers still had less than a high school education, nearly double the national average (see tables 2.6 and 2.8). While not necessarily matched to the experience or interests of job seekers, these jobs do represent reemployment opportunities.

These jobs may also represent the risk of occupational downgrading. Experienced blue-collar workers, in particular, do not qualify for the large number of growing white-collar, professional jobs, and are over-qualified for many other growth sector jobs. Absent retraining and educational upgrading, many will be faced with longer-term unemployment and declining earnings.

To examine these adjustment issues more directly, we first compared the education and training of long-term unemployed workers with those of workers employed in growth and nongrowth sectors of the economy. We selected the long-term unemployed because they account for a growing share of the unemployed and because they represent a reasonable proxy for workers targeted under Title III of JTPA and included in several recent Department of Labor demonstration projects. In these comparisons, we used broad criteria to define the growth sector—a two-digit industry was defined as growing if it had a growth rate at or above the national average between 1979 and 1986.[4] If the unemployed are indeed faced with skill mismatches, the data should reveal large gaps between the human capital attributes of the long-term unemployed and those working in growth sectors.

The results of the comparison highlight two important points (table 2.9). The first is to confirm the sharp divergence between growing and nongrowing industries. It is evident that new job opportunities place a disproportionate emphasis on young workers, those with more education, and jobs in the sales, administrative support, and service fields. Growth sector jobs also employ relatively small shares of prime-age men, semiskilled, and skilled blue-collar workers, groups most affected by recent changes in the structure of job opportunities.

The second point is that, on at least a broad level, the long-term unemployed are not well positioned to compete for jobs in growth sectors. While comparable shares of both groups had high school educations, nearly 19 percent of growth sector employees possessed a college degree, in contrast to 5.7 percent of the long-term unemployed. In fact, in 1985 fully one-third of the long-term unemployed had completed less than high school, more than double the share for growth sector employees.

Table 2.9
**Education, Age, and Occupational Composition by Industry and
Unemployment Status, 1985[a]**

	Growth industries[b]	Other industries	Long-term unemployed[c]	All unemployed
Education				
Less than high school	17.1	21.5	33.6	28.9
High school	41.4	44.4	47.4	45.2
Some college	22.8	17.7	13.3	16.7
College graduate	18.7	16.4	5.7	9.2
Age				
16–19	10.5	3.9	8.4	12.5
20–24	17.7	12.5	20.1	22.2
25–44	51.8	56.4	53.7	50.1
45+	20.0	27.1	17.8	15.2
Sex/age				
Prime-age men	31.1	48.2	39.9	33.7
Prime-age women	32.6	25.8	25.6	27.1
Occupation				
Professional	23.2	20.5	6.4	10.7
Sales	18.9	3.4	10.3	11.9
Administrative	17.2	13.9	8.9	11.9
Service	17.1	9.3	20.4	18.7
Crafts	11.9	16.6	17.4	16.3
Semiskilled	11.7	36.3	36.6	30.5

a. Data cover private, nonagricultural wage and salary workers aged 16 to 61. Calculations by authors based on March Supplements to the Current Population Survey.

b. See appendix 2-A for a definition of growth sectors.

c. Includes workers with 27 or more weeks of unemployment.

A similar scenario emerges on an occupational basis. Just over 23 percent of all growth sector employees held professional jobs in comparison to 6.4 percent for the long-term unemployed. The single largest occupational group among the long-term unemployed was semiskilled positions (36.6 percent). This occupational category accounted for only 11.7 percent of growth sector employment.

If less educated, lower skilled workers are experiencing adjustment difficulties, we would also expect to observe declines in their earnings and increases in their durations of unemployment. Earlier in this chapter, we examined this for semiskilled workers and found such results. We also calculated results for those with less than a high school diploma and those with at least a college degree (table 2.10). Take unemployment first. In 1970, 14.7 percent of all unemployed workers without a high school diploma were jobless for at least 27 weeks. This increased to 17.3 percent in 1979 while in 1985 it rose to 23.7 percent, representing a 61 percent increase over the 15-year period. In contrast, over the same period long-term unemployment among college graduates increased by only 1.6 percentage points, from 11.3 percent to 12.9 percent.

A similar pattern emerges with respect to real earnings. Using 1985 dollars, the real earnings of full-time workers with at least a college degree declined modestly between 1970 and 1985, from $33,472 to $31,472. In contrast, full-time workers with less than 12 years of education experienced a real earnings decline of nearly 16 percent; their average, inflation-adjusted earnings dropped from $15,616 in 1970 to $13,124 in 1985.

To place this in another light, consider the representation of each group in the lowest quartile of the full-time, private, nonagricultural wage and salary distribution.[5] As expected, the share of less educated workers in the lowest wage and salary quartile increased from 31.8 percent in 1970 to 43.1 percent in 1985, with most of the increase occurring after 1979. For those with at least a college degree, there was actually movement out of the lowest quartile.

These results have two important policy implications. First, they indicate that the human capital distribution of job opportunities has become more polarized over time. There has been a large-scale replacement of semiskilled, goods-producing, jobs with professional and sales opportunities requiring relatively high levels of education. To a lesser extent, there has also been a visible shift toward lower level jobs as well. These changes are evident in all industry groups, and especially in the growing service sector. The general outlook for intersector mobility is, at best, difficult. For many workers, the outcome of these changes has been increases in unemployment and declines in real earnings.

Second, the data also suggest significant skills mismatches between the long-term unemployed and growth sectors of the economy. On average, growth industries do not have many jobs that appear to rely

Table 2.10
Unemployment and Earnings Status by Selected Educational Levels[a]

	Less than high school				College or more			
	1970	1974	1979	1985	1970	1974	1979	1985
All Workers								
Percent long-term unemployed	14.7	15.4	17.3	23.7	11.3	12.9	10.2	12.9
Percent in lowest full-time earnings quartile	31.8	34.8	37.5	43.1	11.1	12.6	11.4	9.6
Annual mean earnings full-time workers (1985 $)	15,617	15,403	14,744	13,124	33,346	30,875	28,900	31,472
Prime-Age Men								
Percent long-term unemployed	11.6	17.8	19.6	30.5	10.6	18.9	13.3	16.9
Percent in lowest full-time earnings quartile	11.3	12.4	16.1	26.4	3.6	5.4	5.4	4.9
Annual mean earnings, full-time workers (1985 $)	20,758	21,106	20,347	16,790	38,862	36,660	34,402	37,307

a. Data cover private, nonagricultural wage and salary workers aged 16 to 61. Calculations by authors based on March Supplements to the Current Population Survey.

on the skills and education of long-term unemployed workers. While there are indeed some jobs like this, they represent a proportionately small share of all growth sector jobs. For many of the long-term unemployed, a return to slow growing or declining industries may represent the best avenue to obtain jobs that require their skills. But obtaining a job in this sector can, almost by definition, be quite time consuming and risky. Unless workers are willing to wait for such jobs to develop, they will be faced with having to choose between making an investment in retraining and education or accepting a lower-wage job. Since most workers would prefer not to accept a drop in earnings, it is critical to identify the importance and feasibility of their obtaining a comparable-wage job.

The Changing Structure of Wage Opportunities

Maintaining comparable earnings can be important for several reasons. Perhaps most important is that earnings loss can have harmful and lasting effects on individuals and their families. The literature on plant closings and worker displacement is replete with evidence showing the economic and personal hardships of sudden and sustained earnings declines. These considerations alone suggest the desirability of federal policies that facilitate reemployment at comparable wages.

Policy should also be based on an assessment of whether earnings loss represents a problem of economic efficiency, however. It could be that displaced workers have been selectively laid off because they are less productive than other workers with similar skills and abilities. If this is the case, then much of their observed earnings decline can be viewed as a market-wage adjustment, not an efficiency problem. Similarly, the existence of interindustry wage differences for equally skilled workers, or economic rents, can also be used to explain earnings declines. Efficiency wage theories, as they are called, view such differentials as efficient, insofar as they represent differences in industry-specific decisions regarding profit maximization.[6] Since most industries paying relatively high wages are in the goods-producing sector, and because this sector has accounted for a disproportionate share of displaced workers, earnings loss can also be seen as the result of moving from a high- to a low-rent industry. While such a result will adversely affect a worker, it will not necessarily represent an inefficient allocation of workers. Workers will have become reemployed in industries that offer wages commensurate with their skills and abilities.

Under either scenario, the case for reemployment at comparable wages is weakened. Since the outcome of the reemployment process is viewed as efficient, limited economic benefits can be derived by helping workers fully recoup their earnings loss. From a policy perspective then, the question becomes whether, on the basis of equity considerations, society should bear the cost of helping workers make up what were otherwise economic rents.

While economic rents may explain some of the earnings loss experienced by displaced workers, there is reason to believe that they are insufficient in size to account for the majority of the loss. For one thing, selective layoff is most plausible for white-collar workers. High rates of unionization and the prevalence of seniority rules among blue-collar workers protect them from complete employer discretion during a layoff. In addition, not all displaced workers lose jobs from high-rent industries. Over 30 percent of workers losing their jobs between 1981 and 1986 were displaced from the service sector, and another 8 percent from the transportation, utilities, and communication industries; each of these industry groups and especially the service sector have been shown to pay wages that are lower than those offered in all other industries, after controlling for differences in human capital and personal characteristics.[7] Even among blue-collar workers, whose wages have historically been boosted by union membership, only 30 percent actually belong to a union. And in the manufacturing sector, roughly 55 percent of blue-collar workers do not belong to a union.[8] It is thus difficult to argue that the majority of a displaced worker's earnings loss is attributable to market-wage adjustments or the loss of economic rents.[9]

In light of this, one way to assess the importance of comparable-wage employment is by comparing the reemployment earnings of displaced workers with those of other similar workers. If the displaced become reemployed at earnings levels below those of other workers with like skills and abilities, and if these differences persist over time, then a reasonable case can be made for federal policies that emphasize reemployment at comparable wages. Indeed, several studies have shown that displacement leads to earnings loss; however, data limitations and the infrequent use of comparison groups make their findings inconclusive. This is especially so regarding the duration of earnings decline. Some studies have estimated that up to 50 percent of observed earnings losses are eliminated within two years, while others have shown that such declines persist over time.[10]

To address these issues, we relied on earnings information from a nationally representative sample of adult workers included in the January 1986 Current Population Survey. Since this sample also identifies workers who were permanently dislocated from their jobs between 1981 and 1986, it can be used to determine how the reemployment earnings of displaced workers compare with those of other workers with similar characteristics. The data can also be used to observe the time pattern of earnings loss and how earnings loss may vary among subgroups of the population.

To assess the effect of dislocation on earnings, we estimated a regression model for all employed men between the ages of 20 and 61 using the log of January 1986 weekly earnings as the dependent variable, and a standard set of demographic characteristics, along with education, occupation, and industry variables, as controls.[11] Alternative versions of a dummy variable reflecting one's displacement status were used to directly observe the effect of displacement. These variables were designed to identify the average percentage effect of dislocation on earnings, its pattern over time, and any differences between blue- and white-collar workers, and those affected by plant closings and other types of layoff. This basic model was estimated separately using three sample specifications to determine the sensitivity of the findings.

Because of data limitations, the model could be estimated accurately only for all workers. Regional models were prohibited by insufficient sample size, while separate modelling for blue- and white-collar workers was limited by problems in matching up the comparison group. For example, since the nondisplaced do not have a layoff job, they can only be matched with displaced workers in one of two ways; on the basis of their current occupation, or on the basis of each group's current occupation. In the first case, the estimated effect of displacement on earnings will likely be biased downward as a result of having to assume that occupational requirements remained stable between the year of layoff and January 1986. Over a short period of time, this assumption would be reasonable; however, since large proportions of the displaced lost their jobs as far back as 1981 and 1982, making such an assumption is tenuous given the occupational and educational upgrading discussed earlier in the chapter.

In the second case, underestimates of the effects of displacement are also likely since the majority of displaced workers do not experience interoccupational mobility, a major cause of earnings loss. As a result, selecting on the basis of current occupation would produce a sample of dislocated workers who became reemployed largely in the same field from which they were laid off. Thus, the results presented here below pertain only to the average worker. Questions relating to the time pattern of earnings effects by subgroup and region will have to await the availability of additional data.

Overall, our results show that when displaced workers become reemployed, they do earn less than other workers with similar characteristics (table 2.11). Depending on the sample used, the earnings difference ranges from 15 to 20 percent, and holds even after controlling for differences in hours worked; the mean hourly wage effect of displacement is nearly identical to the total earnings effect, suggesting that the relatively low earnings of the displaced is not the result of working less.

The results also reveal three other important findings. First, white- as well as blue-collar workers appear to earn less than others with similar characteristics, although the impact for blue-collar workers tends, as expected, to be slightly greater.[12] Second, the results show that regardless of why a worker was laid off, earnings differences remain large and statistically significant. Those affected by plant closings as well as other types of layoff both earn significantly less than other workers with similar characteristics. One interpretation of this is that the selective layoff view of earnings loss can, at best, be only partially correct. Since employers cannot readily exercise discretion

Table 2.11
Percentage Effects of Dislocation on the January 1986 Weekly Earnings of Private, Nonagricultural Male Workers, Aged 20–61

	(1) Sample: Dislocated workers laid off from full-time jobs and reemployed; other full-time workers	(2) Sample: Dislocated workers laid off from full-time jobs and reemployed in full-time jobs; other full-time workers	(3) Sample: All workers
All dislocated workers	−.190***	−.135***	−.154***
(Mean hourly wage effect)	—	—	−.149***
Layoff Occupation			
White-collar	−.172***	−.126***	−.139***
Blue-collar	−.202***	−.141***	−.164***
Reason for Layoff			
Plant closing	−.206***	−.144***	−.182***
Other	−.170***	−.124***	−.119***
Year of Layoff			
1985	−.286***	−.214***	−.254***
1984	−.191***	−.145***	−.149***
1983	−.221***	−.134***	−.162***
1982	−.123***	−.093***	−.084*
1981	−.101*	−.070	−.078

***Significant at 99 percent

** Significant at 95 percent

* Significant at 90 percent

over who to layoff during a plant shutdown, and because plant closings accounted for well over half of all layoffs, the relatively low earnings of the displaced cannot be wholly attributed to selective layoff on the basis of poor productivity or performance.[13] This is consistent with our earlier discussion of selective layoffs and helps to better explain the economic consequences of earnings loss.

An alternative view is that the relatively large effect of plant closings on earnings loss reflects the elimination of recall opportunities and a greater willingness on the part of displaced workers to accept a drop in their earnings. This is not inconsistent with the above interpretation, and only serves to further highlight the importance and difficulty of obtaining comparable wage jobs.

Third, the findings by year of layoff suggest that earnings loss does diminish over time; losses are greatest for those laid off in 1985 and least for those who lost a job in 1981. However, it appears that it may still take up to two years to recoup 50 percent of the loss. While this suggests that earnings loss is partly transitory, it should not be viewed too optimistically. Five years of substantially lower earnings represents a sizeable and sustained loss to individuals and their families. Moreover, although this pattern may also reflect the effects of the 1980 to 1982 recessions on postlayoff recovery, the results for 1984 alone suggest that a large loss may still persist for at least two years. On the basis of these results, a case can be made to support federal policies that facilitate reemployment at comparable wages.

Given these findings, what can be said about the feasibility of obtaining a comparable-wage job? Part of the answer lies in how the distribution of wages and salaries has changed. If, as many argue, employment opportunities have become increasingly low-wage, then maintaining a mid-level or high-earnings job will be relatively difficult regardless of one's human capital.[14] Human capital can also come into play if the jobs that constitute the wage distribution have changed. If the human capital upgrading we observed earlier has affected the composition of jobs in the wage distribution, then maintaining one's earnings will also be dependent on the extent of skill mismatches and the feasibility of overcoming them.

To assess the changing distribution of job opportunities, we divided the annual wage and salary income of workers into quartiles, using the 1970 distribution as the base.[15] All dollars were then expressed in 1985 values, and used to examine two aspects of the changing structure of wage opportunities, including the distribution itself, and the contribution of employment in each wage and salary quartile to total employment change between 1970 and 1974, 1974 and 1979, and 1979 and 1985. To assess the effect of growing part-time employment on the distribution, we also computed estimates for full-time and all workers, separately. The earnings cut-offs for both groups of workers are presented below.

Considering the wage and salary distribution first, our findings show overall stability with a slight rise at the tails (table 2.12). On average, it does not appear that among working age, private, nonagricultural workers, there has been a sharp downward shift in *the distribution* of wages and salaries. Among all workers, the data indicate a slight rise

Annual Earnings Quartiles for Full-Time and All Workers
(1985 dollars)

	Full-time workers				All workers			
	Lowest quartile	Low-middle quartile	High-middle quartile	Highest quartile	Lowest quartile	Low-middle quartile	High-middle quartile	Highest quartile
Earnings Range	<$9,735	$9,735–$16,000	$16,001–$26,000	>$26,000	<$5,510	$5,510–$13,000	$13,000–$23,200	>$23,200

in the proportion employed in the lower and upper tails of the distribution, with a small decline in the middle. This is likely due to the increasing share of part-time employment, since the distribution for just full-time workers exhibited a small upward trend between 1970 and 1985.

Changes in the distribution of wages and salaries is only a crude indicator of the direction that employment is taking. A more informative indicator is the contribution of employment in each quartile of the distribution to total employment change. This measure provides a clearer indication of how jobs are changing and the direction that the total distribution may take.

Estimates of this measure show that the shifting pattern of employment growth and decline has placed a disproportionate emphasis on the growth of low- *and* high-wage jobs. Opportunities in the middle of the distribution appear to be a smaller part of the large number of jobs that have grown in recent years. Between 1979 and 1985, the contribution of jobs in the middle of the distribution declined relative to the previous period's rapid expansion. At the same time, employment growth at the tails of the distribution accelerated. While the overall distribution of wages and salaries may not have changed substantially, it is clear that since 1979 there has been a growing emphasis placed on low- and high-wage work at the expense of jobs in the middle.

This pattern of changing wage opportunities is consistent with the pattern of industry growth and decline. For the past 16 years, and especially since 1979, the economy has increasingly emphasized industries paying relatively low-wages (table 2.13). This is evident from earnings comparisons between industries defined as growing and those experiencing below-average growth rates between 1979 and 1986. In

Table 2.12
Wage and Salary Distribution of Private, Nonagricultural Workers, Aged 16 to 61, by wage quartile[a]

	All wage and salary workers				Full-time wage and salary workers			
	1	2	3	4	1	2	3	4
Percent Distribution								
1970	25.0	25.0	25.0	25.0	25.0	25.0	25.0	25.0
1974	25.9	24.9	23.4	25.7	24.7	23.5	26.4	25.9
1979	24.8	27.2	23.1	24.9	25.1	23.8	22.5	22.9
1985	24.9	26.9	23.1	25.1	24.7	26.9	25.8	26.2
Net Shares of Employment Growth[b]								
1970–1974	26.3	25.2	8.8	39.6	28.5	8.7	9.2	53.9
1974–1979	14.1	48.3	20.4	16.9	21.1	67.6	7.2	13.9
1979–1985	25.5	24.9	23.1	26.5	22.4	22.1	26.6	29.0

a. Calculations by authors based on March Supplements to the Current Population Survey.
b. Net shares were calculated by dividing employment change in each quartile by total employment change for each time period, separately.

Table 2.13
Comparisons of Earnings Between Growing and Nongrowing Industries (1985)[a]

	Growing industries[b]	Nongrowing industries
Mean Annual Earnings		
All workers	$15,299	$19,884
Full-time workers	18,919	21,742
Distribution of		
Earnings Among		
Full-Time Wage		
and Salary Workers		
Lowest quartile	27.4	20.6
Low-middle quartile	27.6	22.8
High-middle quartile	22.3	24.2
Highest quartile	22.7	32.3

a. Data cover private, nonagricultural wage and salary workers aged 16 to 61. Calculations by authors based on March Supplements to the Current Population Survey.

b. See appendix 2-A for a description of growth industries.

1985, for example, the mean earnings of full-time wage and salary workers employed in the growth sector was $18,919, compared to $21,742 for those working in nongrowth sectors. Moreover, 27.4 percent of workers in growth industries were employed in the lowest quartile of the wage and salary distribution in contrast to 20.6 percent of employees in nongrowing industries.[16]

Similar differences are evident when comparing the goods-producing sector and the rapidly expanding service sector (table 2.14). Two important points emerge here. The first is that service industries historically have had a disproportionate concentration of employment in the low end of the distribution, although their relative earnings position has improved somewhat over time. For example, roughly 30 percent of employment in goods production has been in the highest quartile of the wage distribution, in comparison to no more than 23 percent of service sector employment. Since service-producing industries have accounted for most of the increase in employment after 1979, it follows that job generation would emphasize lower-wage employment.

The second point is that the declining share of jobs in the middle of the distribution appears attributable to a slowdown in both goods production and service employment. While the large drop in goods-pro-

Table 2.14
Distribution of Employment Shares by Wage Quartile and Industry Sector, All Workers[a]

	Goods-producing industries				Service-producing industries			
	1	2	3	4	1	2	3	4
Percent Distribution								
1970	13.5	24.0	30.2	30.0	34.2	25.4	20.9	19.1
1974	14.5	23.0	28.0	34.2	33.1	26.1	20.3	20.1
1979	13.2	24.4	27.0	35.4	31.8	28.7	20.8	18.5
1985	13.4	24.7	27.4	34.4	30.4	27.9	21.1	20.6
Percentage Contribution to Employment Change								
1970–1974	33.8	5.0	−12.2	75.5	24.1	32.5	15.0	28.5
1974–1979	−10.9	48.1	7.7	53.8	22.0	47.5	24.1	6.5
1979–1985	6.9	3.5	13.8	−124.1	24.7	24.2	22.1	28.9
1970–1985	12.0	31.2	0.0	57.0	23.9	31.9	21.2	23.1

a. Data cover private, nonagricultural wage and salary workers aged 16 to 61. Calculations by authors based on March Supplements to the Current Population Survey.

ducing employment since 1979 was concentrated in the upper end of the distribution, the growth of middle-wage jobs dropped significantly. Moreover, employment growth in the service sector was driven largely by an expansion in the contribution of low- and high-wage work; the net contribution of jobs in the middle of the distribution also declined relative to other periods.

The downward trend in the wage distribution of growing jobs helps to explain why so many workers affected by recent economic changes have experienced earnings declines. The rapid growth of jobs at both ends of the wage distribution has left many unemployed semiskilled and prime-age male workers with new opportunities that require a move either up or down the earnings ladder. Since these workers do not qualify readily for high-wage jobs, and because the growth of mid-level jobs has declined, their most likely source of new opportunities lies in the low-wage sector.[17]

The wage and salary distribution of prime-age men, semiskilled workers, and the less educated confirm this (table 2.15). Throughout the 1970s, these groups experienced a steady decline in their earnings; after 1979, however, the decline was substantially accelerated. Reflecting changes in the composition of employment, women, professional workers, and the better educated were able to move up the earnings ladder.

But the problem faced by workers most affected by recent economic changes is not just one of a growing polarization in the wage distribution of new employment opportunities. Large changes have also occurred in the composition of employment within each wage and salary quartile. Overall, we find a substantial degree of occupational and educational upgrading within the wage and salary distribution (table 2.16).

In each wage quartile, there has been a steady increase in the representation of better educated and trained workers. This is especially evident at the higher ends of the distribution where prime-age men and semiskilled workers have lost ground. There is also a consistent decline in the representation of employment in goods production, also particularly evident in the upper end of the distribution. Even in the low-middle quartile, we see the increasing emphasis placed on service

Table 2.15
Wage and Salary Distribution of Selected Worker Subgroups, All Workers[a]
(Row Percentages)

	1970				1974				1979				1985			
	1	2	3	4	1	2	3	4	1	2	3	4	1	2	3	4
Sex/Age																
Prime-age men	3.6	12.7	32.4	51.4	4.6	12.1	28.7	54.6	4.9	13.9	27.3	53.9	7.1	18.0	27.2	47.7
Prime-age women	33.3	39.6	22.4	4.7	30.8	38.7	24.3	6.2	26.6	39.5	25.8	8.1	24.7	32.2	27.0	13.1
Education																
Less than high school diploma	33.7	27.1	23.9	15.3	36.8	25.8	21.5	15.9	39.4	27.8	18.6	14.2	43.5	30.1	16.7	9.8
More than college degree	11.7	13.3	17.4	57.6	12.1	16.1	19.5	52.3	11.7	16.5	22.2	49.5	9.7	15.3	22.4	52.6
Occupation																
Professional	10.2	14.3	23.2	52.3	10.0	15.2	23.2	51.6	10.7	17.7	26.1	45.5	8.9	16.7	25.6	48.9
Semiskilled	23.0	30.7	29.5	16.8	24.1	28.9	27.5	19.6	21.5	30.1	26.5	21.9	25.1	32.6	24.3	18.0

a. Data cover private, nonagricultural wage and salary workers aged 16 to 61. Calculations by authors based on March Supplements to the Current Population Survey.

Table 2.16
Education, Industry, and Occupational Distribution by Wage and
Salary Quartile, All Wage and Salary Workers[a]

	Low-middle quartile				High-middle quartile			
	1970	1974	1979	1985	1970	1974	1979	1985
Education								
Less than high school diploma	38.7	30.8	25.6	20.7	34.2	27.3	20.1	13.4
High school diploma	44.3	46.5	48.6	49.3	45.7	47.2	47.8	46.2
Some college	12.3	15.2	17.9	19.6	13.8	16.0	19.5	23.0
College degree or more	4.8	7.4	7.9	10.2	6.3	9.5	12.6	17.4
Industry								
Goods-producing	39.5	36.4	34.0	29.9	49.9	47.3	44.0	38.5
Service-producing	60.5	63.6	66.0	70.1	50.1	52.7	56.0	61.5
Occupation								
Professional	9.4	10.3	11.9	13.9	15.3	16.9	20.8	24.8
Admin. support	23.4	24.1	24.3	21.6	20.2	20.0	20.9	21.1
Semiskilled	34.0	30.9	26.9	23.6	32.8	31.4	27.9	20.5
Sales	9.6	10.0	10.5	12.2	7.8	8.3	8.1	10.7
Service	13.6	14.2	15.7	15.9	5.4	5.3	5.4	5.3

	Low-wage quartile				High-wage quartile			
	1970	1974	1979	1985	1970	1974	1979	1985
Education								
Less than high school diploma	46.2	42.4	39.6	32.3	22.2	18.5	14.2	7.2
High school diploma	33.5	35.0	35.4	40.0	39.6	39.7	39.6	33.5
Some college	16.3	17.4	18.8	20.7	17.1	18.6	20.2	21.6
College degree or more	4.0	5.3	6.2	7.0	21.0	23.2	26.0	37.6
Industry								
Goods-producing	21.6	22.3	20.1	17.5	53.6	52.5	53.5	44.5
Service-producing	78.4	77.7	79.9	82.5	46.4	47.5	46.5	55.5
Occupation								
Professional	6.4	6.6	7.9	7.9	35.3	34.4	33.8	43.5
Semiskilled	24.5	24.8	21.1	19.5	19.2	20.5	21.5	13.9
Sales	15.4	15.1	16.4	19.3	12.6	11.5	10.7	13.5
Service	23.9	26.3	28.5	27.3	1.6	1.5	1.4	1.4

a. Data cover private, nonagricultural wage and salary workers aged 16 to 61. Calculations by authors based on March Supplements to the Current Population Survey.

employment and jobs that require more education and occupational preparation. As workers in each quartile lose their jobs, obtaining comparable wages will depend on how prepared they are to meet greater educational and skill requirements.

If workers cannot obtain comparable-wage jobs within their old industries, it is clear that they will be faced with two interrelated problems. The first is the growth in the contribution of low-wage employment to total job expansion. The changing structure of wage opportunities is such that reemployment in a growth sector will increase the likelihood of an earnings decline. The second problem will be the need to overcome educational and possibly occupational training deficiencies in response to upgrading within each quartile of the wage and salary distribution. As one moves up the distribution, these deficiencies appear to increase in magnitude, suggesting that relatively large investments in training and education would have to be made in those workers losing high-wage jobs.

Changing Regional Employment Opportunities

Although national trends in the structure of job opportunities influence worker adjustment patterns, it is ultimately at the regional level where such adjustments take place. If the rate and nature of economic change were uniformly distributed among regions, then one would not expect to observe large variations in regional adjustment. However, as has been well documented, strong differences in economic growth have developed in recent years, especially since 1979 (table 2.17). These differences have contributed to an uneven pattern of regional adjustment to change. For the most part, those regions experiencing sluggish growth have also experienced relatively high rates and long durations of unemployment.

Differences in regional adjustment patterns have also been influenced by sharp variations in the changing structure of job opportunities. The changing nature of human capital requirements and wage opportunities has been much more pronounced in some regions than others, exacerbating the adjustment problems faced by workers.

This is illustrated with information on the nature of changing job

Table 2.17
Selected Economic Indicators by Region and Year[a]

	Percent long-term unemployed				Percentage increase in long-term unemployed, 1979–85	Percent change in employment, 1979–85
	1970	1974	1979	1985		
U.S.	12.9	13.7	14.1	20.4	44.7	16.1
New England	13.4	16.4	16.2	15.5	−4.3	10.2
Mid-Atlantic	14.5	17.0	19.4	23.2	19.6	9.4
East North Central	12.1	14.7	14.4	23.5	63.2	3.8
West North Central	11.3	12.6	11.8	19.7	66.9	5.4
South Atlantic	9.3	11.0	13.7	17.7	29.2	26.9
East South Central	11.8	9.1	13.2	23.9	81.2	13.7
West South Central	12.0	10.1	10.9	20.9	91.7	28.0
Mountain	13.1	8.8	10.1	17.4	72.3	29.0
Pacific	16.2	15.9	12.4	17.7	42.7	19.9

a. Data cover private, nonagricultural wage and salary workers aged 16 to 61. Calculations by authors based on March Supplements to the Current Population Survey.

opportunities in regions with similar types of employment declines, but vastly different unemployment rates—the East North Central states and the Mid-Atlantic states (table 2.18).[18] These two regions experienced significant declines in their shares of goods-producing jobs, and particularly manufacturing jobs. Moreover, both regions also underwent sharp decreases in semiskilled jobs and occupations. On the surface, these results would appear to be at odds with the fact that unemployment in 1986 was much higher in the East North Central states than it was in the Mid-Atlantic states. But a closer look at variations in the contribution to changing job opportunities provides a somewhat clearer picture and helps to clarify why the two regions have had different patterns of adjustment.

In the Mid-Atlantic states, the changing nature of job opportunities was much more evenly distributed than in the East North Central states. While the direction of change was the same in both regions, the Mid-Atlantic states did not experience such a substantial upheaval in the nature of available job opportunities. As a result, it is quite feasible that reemployment opportunities in this region were not nearly as constrained (or polarized) as in the East North Central states, providing workers with substantially more flexibility and choice.

As an example, consider the occupational and educational changes

Table 2.18
Changing Job Opportunities in the East North Central and Mid-Atlantic States[a/b]

| | East North Central States | | | | | | |
| | Distribution | | | | Percentage contribution to net new employment | | |
	1970	1974	1979	1985	1970–74	1974–79	1979–85
Industry							
Goods-producing	46.0	43.9	43.5	35.5	−3.1	35.6	−172.9
Manufacturing	40.4	38.5	37.5	29.7	−1.6	16.4	−172.9
Service-producing	53.7	55.7	56.3	64.3	100.0	67.1	274.6
Services	14.5	15.3	16.9	21.5	32.8	47.9	142.4
Occupation							
Professional	15.9	15.6	16.6	20.6	9.5	35.5	108.5
Sales	11.1	10.3	9.9	12.7	−6.3	3.9	71.4
Admin. supp./clerical	16.3	16.5	16.2	15.9	22.2	9.2	10.0
Priv. and prof. services	2.7	2.2	1.4	1.8	−9.5	−13.2	8.6
Other services	10.8	12.1	12.9	12.9	39.7	27.6	14.3
Crafts	13.4	13.7	14.7	13.2	19.0	34.2	−18.6
Unskilled	29.3	29.2	27.8	22.5	25.4	2.6	−92.9
Education							
Less than high school diploma	35.8	29.5	24.9	18.3	−107.6	−65.8	−117.1
High school diploma	42.7	45.4	46.5	45.4	103.0	68.4	22.4
Some college	13.4	14.9	17.3	20.4	47.0	64.5	84.2
College degree or more	8.1	10.3	11.3	16.0	57.6	31.6	113.2

| | Mid-Atlantic States | | | | | | |
| | Distribution | | | | Percentage contribution to net new employment | | |
	1970	1974	1979	1985	1970–74	1974–79	1979–85
Industry							
Goods-producing	41.0	38.5	37.1	30.0	−325.0	9.8	−45.8
Manufacturing	35.1	32.6	31.9	24.0	−337.5	17.7	−60.2
Service-producing	58.7	61.0	62.5	69.5	425.0	90.3	144.9
Services	16.5	19.2	20.7	25.9	425.0	50.0	81.4
Occupation							
Professional	17.7	19.5	19.7	24.7	200.0	23.3	74.0
Sales	11.0	9.9	11.3	13.3	−100.0	38.3	33.1
Admin. supp./clerical	18.6	18.3	19.5	17.8	−16.7	45.0	1.0
Priv. and prof. serv.	2.5	2.4	1.7	1.7	−8.3	−13.2	1.6
Other services	9.6	11.0	12.0	12.4	150.0	31.7	15.7
Crafts	12.7	13.4	12.2	11.8	83.3	−10.0	7.1
Unskilled	27.3	25.1	23.1	18.0	−191.7	−18.3	−33.1
Education							
Less than high school diploma	34.7	28.8	23.2	16.9	−282.6	−87.1	−56.8
High school diploma	41.6	42.6	45.6	43.8	91.3	106.5	22.5
Some college	13.0	15.4	17.0	18.4	139.1	48.4	35.1
College degree or more	10.7	13.3	14.2	20.9	152.2	32.3	99.1

a. Data refer to workers aged 16 to 61 employed in private, nonagricultural wage and salary distribution. Calculations are based on the March Supplements to the Current Population Survey.
b. The states comprising these two regions include: 1. East North Central—Ohio, Indiana, Illinois, Michigan and Wisconsin; 2. Mid-Atlantic—New York, New Jersey and Pennsylvania.

in employment. In the East North Central region, nearly all net new employment was in professional jobs and for individuals with at least a college degree. In fact, the decline in semiskilled work and employment among the least educated was just about equal to the total level of employment expansion. For these workers, reemployment opportunities are constrained not only by an insufficient demand, but also by the nature of new opportunities.

While a similar pattern is evident in the Mid-Atlantic region, it is not nearly as pronounced. The (negative) contribution of all blue-collar employment in the Mid-Atlantic region was only half that of the East North Central region, as was the decline in employment among the least educated. And although professional employment accounted for a disproportionately large share of total growth, it was also much less than in the East North Central region. Thus, while workers in the Mid-Atlantic states faced a tough road to reemployment, it appears to have been a smoother one to travel. As a result, one would expect labor market adjustment to be more efficient.

This example illustrates how regional variations in the structure of job opportunities can influence worker adjustment to change. At the same time, there have also been large differences in the structure of wage opportunities on a regional basis. The trend toward lower-wage work has been particularly evident in the Midwest region. In the East North Central states, for example, 85 percent of net new employment between 1979 and 1985 was attributable to jobs in the lowest quartile of the wage and salary distribution. Jobs in the second lowest quartile contributed another 43 percent, while the highest paying jobs registered a net loss of just over 53 percent. Following the example presented above, jobs at the bottom and top of the wage and salary distribution accounted for roughly 23 percent of net employment growth in the Mid-Atlantic states, respectively.

The large growth of low-wage jobs in the East North Central states may seem at odds with the rapid growth of employment among college educated, professional workers in that region. However, upon closer inspection, two explanations emerge. First, sales jobs, which represented 71 percent of all new jobs in the East North Central states have a disproportionately large share of part-time employment. In 1985, for example, 31.3 percent of all sales jobs held in the U.S. were part time, compared to 20 percent of total employment. Second, the largest source of job loss in the East North Central states was in the goods-producing sector. This sector, which lost many high-wage jobs, was and remains the dominant industry in the region.

For workers residing in the Midwest, the problem of readjustment can thus be viewed as structural. Sharp changes in the structure of job and wage opportunities have contributed to substantial readjustment difficulties. Given the strong shift toward professional and lower-wage employment, workers are indeed faced with a pressing dilemma. Although reemployment in declining sectors may represent the most viable means to obtain a comparable-wage job, their declining numbers can make such a move quite difficult. And while new jobs are growing, they appear to represent a move down the earnings ladder, unless substantial investments in training and education are made. For the unemployed displaced worker, choosing an appropriate road to recovery can indeed be viewed as a formidable task.

While these results are similar to our national findings, they also show how important regional economic conditions are to successful worker adjustment. Some regions, like the Midwest, offer limited alternatives to long-term unemployment, declining earnings, and the prospect of de-skilling. The rate and nature of economic change is so great that workers (and programs to aid them) have no choice but to pursue reemployment alone, almost regardless of wages and skill matching. In other regions where economic change has not been as swift, workers have more flexibility and choice in selecting a reemployment strategy. Programs and policies in these regions might rightly look quite different from those in more hard-hit areas of the country.

To obtain a better understanding of appropriate policy responses to recent economic changes, we turn in the next chapter to an examination of how displaced workers have responded to the challenge of a changing labor market. Our objective is to determine more clearly the extent and nature of potential skill mismatches and the feasibility of policies that pursue as their goal reemployment in comparable-wage jobs.

NOTES

1. To be counted in this quartile, an individual had to have annual earnings of at least $26,000, expressed in 1985 dollars.

2. A similar result emerged for jobs in the second and third quartile of the wage and salary distribution, or among what might be referred to as middle-class jobs. Between 1979 and 1985, these jobs also experienced large shifts in their distribution across educational levels, industries, and occupations. This is discussed more fully later in this chapter.

3. A portion of the shift toward better educated workers reflects the aging of the population, as older, less educated workers retire, and new young college graduates increase their share of total employment. This does not, however, change the implications for worker adjustment. The same general point holds for the findings in table 2.9.

4. See appendix 2-A for a description of how the growth sector was defined.

5. Setting the distribution in 1970 and adjusting wages to 1985 values, the upper end of the low-wage quartile is $9,735. See pages 34 and 35 for a more detailed discussion of the wage and salary distribution.

6. See: Alan Krueger and Lawrence Summers, "Efficiency Wages and the Inter-Industry Wage Structure," *Econometrica* 56, 2(March, 1988).

7. See: Krueger and Summers, "Efficiency Wages," pages 281–287 for estimates of wage differentials by three-digit industry.

8. See: Richard Freeman and James Medoff, *What Do Unions Do?* New York: Basic Books, 1984.

9. A recent study empirically evaluated these issues and found evidence indicating that the loss of economic rents represents only a small portion of the earnings decline experienced by displaced workers. In addition, the same study found that the case for selective layoff is indeed primarily applicable to white-collar workers. While the earnings of blue-collar workers prior to layoff were comparable to those of other workers, predisplacement earnings for white-collar and service workers were lower than those of other similar workers, but not nearly as low as earnings observed on the reemployment job. See: Adam Seitchik, "Labor Displacement in the New Family Economy," Ph.D. diss., Boston University, Boston, MA, August 1988.

10. See: Louis S. Jacobson, "A Tale of Employment Decline in Two Cities: How Bad Was the Worst of Times?" *Industrial and Labor Relations Review* 37, 4 (July 1984); Louis S. Jacobson, "Earnings Losses of Workers Displaced from Manufacturing Industries," in *The Impact of International Trade and Investment on Employment*, Washington, DC: GPO, pp. 87–98, William G. Dewald, ed., 1978; Michael Podgursky and Paul Swaim, "Job Displacement and Earnings Loss: Evidence From the Displaced Worker Survey," *Industrial and Labor Relations Review* 41, 1 (October 1987); Christopher J. Ruhm, "The Economic Consequences of Labor Mobility," *Industrial and Labor Relations Review* 41, 1 (October 1987).

11. While it would have been preferable to also control for tenure and layoff earnings, these data were not available for the nondisplaced group of workers. The regular monthly CPS does not collect tenure information and captures data only for the particular survey month.

12. As discussed earlier, some of the earnings loss experienced by white-collar workers is likely due to selective layoff and reflective of a market-wage adjustment.

13. It is possible, however, for employers to redeploy "the best workers" to other plants within the corporate structure. While this is certainly feasible, it would have to account for the majority of reported plant closings to be consistent with the selective layoff argument. In addition, it is also possible that observed effects of mass layoffs and other types of reductions in force reflect

selective layoff since in these instances employers do have discretion over how to layoff. However, judgment of this is critically dependent on whether the predisplacement earnings of those workers was lower than those of other similar employees, holding other factors constant. As discussed earlier, such a result was found only for white-collar workers, and even in this case, the predisplacement earnings differences were much smaller than those observed during the postlayoff period. Moreover, holding other factors constant, the selective layoff interpretation would predict little, if any, earnings differences between the current earnings of displaced and other similar workers. As shown in table 2.12, just the opposite is observed.

14. For a critical review of recent research on the changing pattern of wage opportunities see: Gary W. Loveman and Chris Tilly, "Good Jobs or Bad Jobs: What Does the Evidence Say?" *New England Economic Review* (January, February, 1988).

15. We chose to rely on quartiles rather than the more familiar thirds to avoid having to arbitrarily select earnings cut-offs and to be able to better examine the distribution. This choice, combined with restricting the analysis to only private, nonagricultural workers between the ages of 16 and 61, should be expected to produce results different from those focused on all wage and salary workers and using thirds to examine the distribution of wages and salaries.

16. An alternative explanation of these earnings differences is that they reflect differences in the position of each sector's workers on the age-earnings profile. Since growing industries, such as services, employ younger and less experienced workers than declining or slow-growing industries, one would expect lower average earnings. We tested for this and found that, after controlling for age, human capital, and other personal characteristics, the service sector pays anywhere between 24 and 36 percent less than any other industry sector. See table 2B in the appendix for the results.

17. This also helps to explain why these worker groups have experienced a decline in their share of high wage jobs despite an overall rise in the share of such jobs nationally.

18. The East North Central includes Ohio, Indiana, Illinois, Michigan, and Wisconsin. The Mid-Atlantic includes New York, New Jersey, and Pennsylvania.

Appendix 2-A Definition of Industry Growth Sector

Definition of Industry Growth Sector

Employment and Earnings reports annual employment levels by detailed industry. From these we are able to calculate secular industry growth rates from the peak year 1979 through the latest year available, 1986. There were only moderate changes in the Standard Industrial Classification system between 1970 and 1980, and we have been able to adjust for most of these in calculating growth from 1979 to 1986.[1] In table 2A-1, growth rates are shown for the 39 two-digit SIC industries, using the 1980 SIC categories.

As shown in table 2A-1, civilian employment grew by 13.1 percent between 1979 and 1986. Industry growth rates were quite varied. In general, manufacturing and agricultural industries were in decline, while almost all other industries grew: construction, transport, communications, utilities, trade, finance, insurance, real estate, and service (other than private household service).

The simplest way to categorize growth sectors of the economy would be to include all expanding industries, or those wherein employment is growing faster than for the nation as a whole. Listing out the sectors experiencing growth, beginning with the fastest growing, we observe the following:

At first glance, there appear to be at least 18 growth industries, wherein employment expanded at a rate in excess of that for the nation. However, "Transportation equipment" is a puzzling case, since the popular conception is that employment in automobile production has declined since its peak in 1979. In fact, the detailed industrial employment figures do show a stagnation in "motor vehicles and motor vehicle equipment," a subset of "Transportation equipment." The "Transportation equipment" sector has grown mostly through the inclusion of a new detailed category, "guided missiles, space vehicles,

51

Rank	Industry	Growth Rate, 1979–86
		percent
1	Business and repair services	71.0
2	Personal services	29.3
3	Finance, insurance, and real estate	28.1
4	Entertainment and recreational services	25.9
5	Health services, except hospitals	25.1
6	Other professional services	24.6
7	Professional & photographic equip., etc.	19.9
8	Forestry and fisheries	19.1
9	Wholesale trade	17.0
10	Printing, publishing, and allied products	16.9
11	Transportation equipment	16.6
12	Public administration	16.6
13	Communications	15.8
14	Retail trade	15.7
15	Construction	15.7
16	Educational and social services	14.7
17	Furniture and fixtures	14.6
18	Hospitals	13.7
	National Employment Growth Rate	13.1
19	Utilities and sanitary services	9.6
20	Transportation	5.1
21	Mining	1.7
22–39	Eighteen Declining Industries	

and parts," which was in all likelihood combined with "miscellaneous manufacturing" under the old SIC categories used in 1979. Therefore, the additional employment reported in "Transportation equipment (manufacturing)" for 1986 is essentially a statistical artifact; we should *not* include this as one of our high-growth categories.

Notice that there are three industries in which there was net employment growth 1979–86, but where expansion was at a rate below the average for the nation. Among these three, the fastest-growing was "Utilities and sanitary services." All five detailed industries within this 2-digit category expanded by at least 5 percent, creating an overall average of almost 10 percent employment growth. In comparison, the next industry down on the list, "Transportation," expanded by only 5 percent.[2] Of the nine detailed industries within Transportation, four grew moderately and five went into decline—not a consistent growth sector in comparison to the 17 above it on the list. After "Transportation" comes "Mining," wherein employment was essentially stagnant. Therefore, it seems that "Utilities and sanitary services," which

53

Table 2A-1
Industry Employment Growth Rates, 1979–86

	Employed civilians (000s)		Percent change 1979–86
	1979	1986	(%)
Total 16+	96,945	109,597	13.1
Agriculture	3,298	3,163	−4.1
Mining	865	880	1.7
Construction	6,299	7,288	15.7
Durable Goods Manufacturing	13,450	12,605	−6.3
Lumber & wood	730	692	−5.2
Furniture & fixtures	567	650	14.6
Stone, clay, etc.	706	616	−12.7
Primary metals	1,262	779	−38.3
Fabricated metals	1,697	1,303	−23.2
Machinery, ex. elec.	2,747	2,503	−8.9
Electrical machinery, etc.	2,293	2,153	−6.1
Transport. equipment	2,298	2,679	16.6
Professional equip., etc.	584	700	19.9
Misc. manufacturing	567	531	−6.3
Nondurable Goods Manufacturing	8,688	8,357	−3.8
Food & kindred products	1,789	1,737	−2.9
Tobacco	64	63	−1.6
Textiles	823	714	−13.2
Apparel, etc.	1,279	1,176	−8.1
Paper, etc.	726	698	−3.9
Printing, etc.	1,507	1,762	16.9
Chemicals, etc.	1,217	1,200	−1.4
Petroleum, etc.	256	169	−34.0
Rubber, etc.	731	688	−5.9
Leather, etc.	275	149	−45.8
Transport, Comm. & P.U.	7,084	7,650	8.0
Transportation	4,384	4,608	5.1
Communications	1,371	1,587	15.8
Utilities & Sanitary	1,328	1,455	9.6
Trade	19,672	22,813	16.0
Wholesale trade	3,775	4,416	17.0
Retail trade	15,898	18,397	15.7
Fire	5,779	7,401	28.1
Services	27,432	34,337	25.2
Private H.H.	1,301	1,241	−4.6
Business & repair	3,362	6,211	71.0
Personal	2,499	3,231	29.3
Entertain. & rec.	1,026	1,292	25.9
Hospitals	3,843	4,368	13.7
Health, ex. hospitals	3,006	3,761	25.1
Educ. & social	8,770	10,062	14.7
Other professional	3,198	3,984	24.6
Forestry & fisheries	157	187	19.1
Public Administration	4,379	5,104	16.6

SOURCE: *Employment and Earnings,* 1/80 and 1/87.

experienced a solid employment expansion, should be included as a high-growth industry, while "Transportation" (and of course "Mining") should be excluded.

By excluding "Transportation equipment" as a statistical aberration and including "Utilities and sanitary services," we end up with 18 growth sectors. Total employment in growth sectors was 66 million in 1979 and 80 million in 1986, an increase of 21.3 percent. Meanwhile, aggregate employment in the remaining sectors (slow-growing and declining) shrunk by 4.8 percent, from 31 million to 29 million. By 1986, almost three out of every four employed civilians were in a growth sector (73.4 percent).

1. Important changes which we have adjusted for are the transfer of the postal service from "public administration" to "transportation," and movement of "ordinance" from "other durable goods industries" into the "fabricated metals" category.

2. SIC terminology can be confusing. "Transportation"—which involves the physical movement of people and goods by surface, air, and water—is one two-digit category, while "Transportation equipment (manufacturing)" is another.

Appendix 2-B
Regression Results of the Effects of
Dislocation on January 1986 Earnings

Table 2B-1
Effects of Dislocation on January 1986 Weekly Earnings
of Private Nonagricultural Male Workers: Sample 1

Dependent variable: Log of current earnings
Sample: Dislocated workers laid off from full-time jobs and reemployed; other full-time workers

	(1)	(2)	(3)	(4)	(5)
Intercept	5.62***	5.62***	5.62***	5.62***	5.61***
	(181.23)	(181.52)	(181.22)	(181.21)	(181.15)
20–24 years of age	−.379***	−.376***	−.379***	−.379***	−.377***
	(−18.17)	(−18.03)	(−18.18)	(−18.16)	(−18.06)
35–44 years of age	.164***	.163***	.164***	.163***	.165***
	(9.58)	(9.55)	(9.58)	(9.56)	(9.68)
45–61 years of age	.192***	.191***	.192***	.192***	.192***
	(11.10)	(11.08)	(11.10)	(11.10)	(11.09)
<12 years education	−.212***	−.212***	−.212***	−.212***	−.210***
	(−10.53)	(−10.51)	(−10.53)	(−10.53)	(−10.43)
>12 years education	.242***	.241***	.242***	.242***	.244***
	(15.45)	(15.38)	(15.42)	(15.44)	(15.55)
White	.199***	.199***	.199***	.199***	.199***
	(9.55)	(9.54)	(9.55)	(9.53)	(9.54)
Blue-collar	−.130***	−.131***	−.130***	−.129***	−.130***
	(−8.07)	(−8.11)	(−8.07)	(−7.89)	(−8.03)
Manufacturing	.211***	.208***	.211***	.211***	.211***
	(10.30)	(10.15)	(10.30)	(10.25)	(10.27)
Other goods	.283***	.276***	.282***	.283***	.283***
	(10.49)	(10.23)	(10.46)	(10.49)	(10.52)
Trade	−.027	−.029	−.027	−.028	−.027
	(−1.24)	(−1.31)	(−1.24)	(−1.28)	(−1.21)
FIRE	.162***	.161***	.162***	.161***	.162***
	(5.09)	(5.06)	(5.10)	(5.07)	(5.11)
TCU	.289***	.286***	.289***	.288***	.289***
	(10.91)	(10.78)	(10.91)	(10.86)	(10.90)
Per. inc. growth	.002***	.002***	.002***	.002***	.002***
(1979–1986)	(2.55)	(2.52)	(2.58)	(2.54)	(2.66)
Dislocated worker	−.190***				
	(−8.86)				
DW x occup. move		−.270***			
		(−9.12)			
DW x same occup.		−.112***			
		(−3.80)			
DW x plant closing			−.206***		
			(−7.34)		
DW x other layoff			−.170***		
			(−5.48)		
DW x blue-collar				−.202***	
				(−7.36)	
DW x white-collar				−.173***	
				(−5.26)	
DW x 1981					−.101*
					(−1.86)
DW x 1982					−.123***
					(−2.91)
DW x 1983					−.221***
					(−4.69)
DW x 1984					−.191***
					(−4.25)
DW x 1985					−.287***
					(−6.71)
R²	.314	.316	.314	.314	.315
F	160.67***	151.41***	150.01***	149.98***	125.75***

NOTE: *t*-statistics in parenthesis
   *** significant at 99%
   ** significant at 95%
   * significant at 90%

Table 2B-2
Effects of Dislocation on January 1986 Weekly Earnings
of Private Nonagricultural Male Workers: Sample 2

Dependent variable: Log of current earnings
Sample: Dislocated workers laid off from full-time jobs and reemployed in full-time jobs; other full-time workers

	(1)	(2)	(3)	(4)	(5)
Intercept	5.63***	5.63***	5.63***	5.63***	5.62***
	(183.39)	(183.58)	(183.37)	(183.37)	(183.25)
20–24 years of age	−.379***	−.377***	−.379***	−.379***	−.377***
	(−18.31)	(−18.23)	(−18.31)	(−18.30)	(−18.22)
35–44 years of age	.163***	.162***	.163***	.162***	.163***
	(9.62)	(9.60)	(9.62)	(9.61)	(9.66)
45–61 years of age	.188***	.188***	.188***	.188***	.188***
	(11.04)	(11.03)	(11.04)	(11.04)	(11.01)
<12 years education	−.208***	−.208***	−.208***	−.208***	−.206***
	(−10.42)	(−10.41)	(−10.42)	(−10.42)	(−10.31)
>12 years education	.239***	.238***	.239***	.239***	.240***
	(15.40)	(15.34)	(15.38)	(15.39)	(15.44)
White	.198***	.198***	.198***	.197***	.198***
	(9.55)	(9.57)	(9.55)	(9.54)	(9.56)
Blue-collar	−.134***	−.134***	−.134***	−.133***	−.134***
	(−8.41)	(−8.43)	(−8.40)	(−8.28)	(−8.38)
Manufacturing	.206***	.204***	.206***	.206***	.206***
	(10.18)	(10.06)	(10.18)	(10.15)	(10.16)
Other goods	.274***	.269***	.274***	.274***	.274***
	(10.25)	(10.06)	(10.23)	(10.25)	(10.23)
Trade	−.025	−.026	−.025	−.025	−.025
	(−1.15)	(−1.19)	(−1.14)	(−1.16)	(−1.14)
FIRE	.161***	.160***	.161***	.161***	.161***
	(5.13)	(5.11)	(5.13)	(5.12)	(5.13)
TCU	.291***	.288***	.291***	.290***	.291***
	(11.10)	(10.99)	(11.09)	(11.07)	(11.08)
Per inc. growth	.002**	.002**	.002**	.002**	.002**
(1979–1986)	(2.51)	(2.49)	(2.53)	(2.50)	(2.60)
Dislocated worker	−.136***				
	(−6.13)				
DW x occup. move		−.204***			
		(−6.60)			
DW x same occup.		−.071***			
		(−2.37)			
DW x plant closing			−.144***		
			(−4.95)		
DW x other layoff			−.125***		
			(−3.90)		
DW x blue-collar				−.142***	
				(−4.97)	
DW x white-collar				−.127***	
				(−3.77)	
DW x 1981					.070
					(−1.24)
DW x 1982					.093**
					(−2.15)
DW x 1983					−.135***
					(−2.77)
DW x 1984					−1.45***
					(−3.13)
DW x 1985					−.214***
					(−4.75)
R²	.311	.312	.311	.311	.312
F	156.70***	147.20***	146.25***	146.24***	122.22***

NOTE: *t*-statistics in parenthesis
    *** significant at 99%
    ** significant at 95%
    * significant at 90%

Table 2B-3
Effects of Dislocation on January 1986 Weekly Earnings
of Private Nonagricultural Male Workers: Sample 3

Dependent variable: Log of current earnings
Sample: All workers

	(1)	(2)	(3)	(4)	(5)	(6)
Intercept	5.54***	5.54***	5.53***	5.54***	5.53***	4.78***
	(162.87)	(163.07)	(162.88)	(162.85)	(162.80)	(118.39)
20–24 years of age	−.518***	−.516***	−.518***	−.518***	−.516***	−.428***
	(−23.42)	(−23.34)	(−23.45)	(−23.42)	(−23.32)	(−20.71)
35–44 years of age	.168***	.167***	.168***	.168***	.169***	.156***
	(8.77)	(8.76)	(8.77)	(8.76)	(8.84)	(8.79)
45–61 years of age	.184***	.184***	.184***	.184***	.184***	.187***
	(9.55)	(9.54)	(9.55)	(9.55)	(9.54)	(10.50)
<12 years education	−.240***	−.239***	−.240***	−.240***	−.238***	−.214***
	(−10.81)	(−10.80)	(−10.81)	(−10.81)	(−10.73)	(−10.40)
>12 years education	.196***	.194***	.195***	.196***	.197***	.187***
	(11.33)	(11.27)	(11.30)	(11.32)	(11.38)	(11.70)
White	.220***	.220***	.220***	.219***	.220***	.173***
	(9.61)	(9.63)	(9.61)	(9.60)	(9.61)	(8.17)
Blue-collar	−.144***	−.144***	−.144***	−.143***	−.143***	−.120***
	(−8.09)	(−8.13)	(−8.10)	(−7.94)	(−8.06)	(−7.29)
Manufacturing	.294***	.291***	.294***	.293***	.293***	.279***
	(13.00)	(12.89)	(13.01)	(12.96)	(12.98)	(13.35)
Other goods	.350***	.344***	.349***	.350***	.350***	.360***
	(11.86)	(11.64)	(11.82)	(11.85)	(11.87)	(13.18)
Trade	−.015	−.016	−.015	−.016	−.015	−.021
	(−0.64)	(−0.68)	(−0.61)	(−0.67)	(−0.62)	(−0.92)
FIRE	.227***	.226***	.227***	.227***	.227***	.235***
	(6.41)	(6.40)	(6.42)	(6.40)	(6.42)	(7.19)
TCU	.336***	.333***	.336***	.335***	.336***	.318***
	(11.54)	(11.43)	(11.55)	(11.50)	(11.54)	(11.81)
Per. inc. growth (1979–1986)	.003***	.003***	.003***	.003***	.003***	.002***
	(3.92)	(3.90)	(3.97)	(3.91)	(4.02)	(3.45)
Dislocated worker	−.154***					−.150***
	(−6.37)					(−6.69)
DW x occup. move		−.233***				
		(−6.99)				
DW x same occup.		−.076***				
		(−2.28)				
DW x plant closing			−.182***			
			(−5.74)			
DW x other layoff			−.119***			
			(−3.40)			
DW x blue-collar				−.164***		
				(−5.29)		
DW x white-collar				−.140***		
				(−3.77)		
DW x 1981					−.078	
					(−1.27)	
DW x 1982					−.085*	
					(−1.73)	
DW x 1983					−.163***	
					(−3.08)	
DW x 1984					−.150***	
					(−2.98)	
DW x 1985					−.254***	
					(−5.31)	
Hours Worked/Week						.019***
						(29.80)
R^2	.315	.317	.316	.315	.316	.415
F	172.39***	162.02***	161.05***	160.89***	134.55***	247.31***

NOTE: *t*-statistics in parenthesis
     *** significant at 99%
     ** significant at 95%
     * significant at 90%

Table 2B-4
Sample Means for Variables Included in Earnings Regressions

	Sample: Dislocated workers laid off from full-time jobs and reemployed; other full-time workers N = 4934		Sample: Dislocated workers laid off from full-time jobs and reemployed in full-time jobs; other full-time workers N = 4882		Sample: All workers N = 5427	
	Mean	Standard deviation	Mean	Standard deviation	Mean	Standard deviation
Hours per week	44.07	9.23	44.26	8.98	42.49	10.98
Dislocated worker	.10	.31	.10	.29	.10	.30
20–24 years of age	.14	.34	.14	.34	.15	.36
35–44 years of age	.25	.43	.25	.43	.24	.43
45–61 years of age	.25	.43	.25	.43	.25	.43
< 12 years education	.15	.35	.15	.35	.15	.36
> 12 years education	.43	.49	.43	.50	.43	.49
White	.89	.31	.89	.31	.89	.32
Blue-collar	.49	.50	.49	.50	.50	.50
Manufacturing	.36	.48	.36	.48	.35	.48
Other goods	.11	.32	.11	.32	.12	.32
Trade	.20	.40	.20	.40	.20	.40
FIRE	.06	.23	.06	.24	.06	.23
TCU	.11	.31	.11	.31	.11	.31
DW x 1981	.01	.12	.01	.11	.01	.12
DW x 1982	.02	.15	.02	.15	.02	.15
DW x 1983	.02	.14	.02	.13	.02	.14
DW x 1984	.02	.15	.02	.14	.02	.14
DW x 1985	.02	.15	.02	.14	.02	.15
DW x occ. move	.05	.22	.05	.21	.05	.22
DW x same occ.	.05	.22	.05	.22	.05	.22
DW x blue-collar	.06	.24	.06	.23	.06	.24
DW x white-collar	.04	.20	.04	.19	.04	.20
Full 1	.10	.31	.10	.29	−.10	.29
Part 1	0.0	0.0	0.0	0.0	<.01	.07
DW x plant closing	.06	.23	.05	.22	.05	.23
DW x other layoff	.05	.21	.04	.20	.04	.21
Log of current earnings	5.99	.55	6.00	.54	5.94	.63
Pers. inc. growth	16.69	9.64	16.72	9.64	16.62	9.59

3
The Road to Recovery

In a recent television documentary on the closing of a forklift plant in Pennsylvania, two workers were filmed discussing their misfortune. One of the workers remarked that they were "dinosaurs," a dying breed of Americans who work with their "hands and their minds." While certainly not extinct, available data do show that the displaced worker is a markedly different breed from the growth-sector worker, or for that matter from the average full-time worker (table 3.1). Naturally, a disproportionate share of the displaced are from declining and slow-growing sectors, specifically manufacturing (48 percent), and transportation, communication, and utilities (8 percent). In comparison, only 31 percent of all full-time workers are employed in manufacturing.

In these and other respects, displaced workers are a reflection of yesterday's workforce—two-thirds are male, nearly 60 percent are blue-collar, 47 percent graduated from high school, and 20 percent had not gone that far. Among the blue-collar displaced, 64 percent are semiskilled.[1] If growth-sector employees represent the worker of the future, the displaced population does not make for a good fit. Within growth sectors, only 22 percent of full-time workers are blue-collar, and most of these are in skilled craft and repair occupations. In addition, almost half of full-time, growth-sector workers are female, only 12 percent have not graduated from high school, and 22 percent have a four-year college degree.

When following the fortunes of these job losers, it is evident that worker displacement is a primary mechanism through which the American economy is making the transition into service sector and white-

61

Table 3.1
Characteristics of Displaced Workers and Other Full-Time Workers[a]

	Workers displaced from full-time jobs	Full-time growth- sector workers[b]	All full-time workers
N (000s)	8,751	37,192	61,420
Industry			
Manufacturing	47.5	—	31.2
Other goods-producing	13.1	13.1	7.9
Transport, comm., util.	7.7	—	8.3
Other service-producing	31.6	86.9	52.6
Occupation			
Executive, professional, and technical	18.4	28.3	26.3
Sales	9.0	18.7	12.6
Administrative support/clerical	9.6	18.2	16.5
Service	5.5	13.2	8.6
Craft and repair (skilled blue-collar)	20.8	12.3	15.2
Semiskilled blue-collar	36.7	9.3	20.9
Sex			
Male	66.3	53.4	59.6
Female	33.7	46.6	40.4
Education			
Not a high school graduate	20.2	12.4	14.3
High school graduate	46.8	42.6	44.0
1–3 years posthigh school	20.1	22.6	21.1
4 years + posthigh school	12.9	22.3	20.5
Wage Quartile on Layoff Job	(Lost job, in 1/86 $)		
<$237/wk (lowest)	29.5	31.0	25.0
$237–350/wk (low middle)	27.2	26.9	25.0
$351–500/wk (high middle)	22.2	22.4	25.0
>500 (highest)	21.1	19.7	25.0

a. Data from the January 1986 Current Population Survey. All data refer to individuals aged 20–61 in January 1986. Displaced workers lost or left a full-time, private, nonagricultural, wage-salary job between January 1981 and January 1986 because of a plant closing, permanent reduction in force, or slack work, without recall as of January 1986.

b. See appendix 2-A for a description of how the growth sector was defined.

collar employment. Certainly, other, more benign mechanisms are also used—early retirement, voluntary turnover, and the emphasis upon technical trades in vocational secondary schools and upgraded educational systems in general. Displacement impresses itself upon us because it is exactly the mechanism which has the potential to create dinosaurs, workers who are caught between the old world of skilled and semiskilled work with "hands and minds" and the new world of the growth sectors.

Displaced workers have several recovery roads from which to choose. One is to find work in a promising new field, in hopes of avoiding a large earnings decline. A successful transition from a declining industry to a growing one at a comparable rate of pay is, of course, most desirable; it serves the broad-based economic goal of flexible adjustment, while limiting the personal suffering of the job loser. But, as we saw in the previous chapter, the educational requirements within growing industries are formidable, particularly at comparable rates of pay. Such an adjustment, although attractive to all in terms of the earnings outcome, is likely to require a large allocation of training and education resources (not to mention the "opportunity cost" of the worker's lost earnings during the retraining period). For policy purposes, this would necessitate a larger commitment to fundamental retraining than that currently available.

A second option is the rapid movement of displaced workers into growth industries and occupations. This can be a risky strategy for many job losers, however, since the earnings distribution in expanding sectors is more clearly determined by educational background than in declining fields. In other words, on average, those with a high school degree or less fare much better in manufacturing than they do in the service-producing sectors. Without an educational upgrade, the movement into growth sectors can result in substantial earnings declines; absent his or her machinery, the formerly high-productivity/ highly-paid manufacturing worker is at risk of becoming a low-productivity/low-paid service worker. While lower-wage reemployment is better than no employment, neither policymakers nor workers are pleased when a high-productivity job is lost and a low-productivity job takes its place. In fact, this is just the kind of transition that a job loser will work to avoid.

For the blue-collar and manufacturing workers who make up a disproportionate fraction of the displacement population, there is a third option—obtaining new jobs in the declining sector from which they were laid off, or at least in a familiar blue-collar setting. At first blush, this option may not appear favorable, since the long-term prognosis in manufacturing is continued decline. The search for a new, comparable-wage job in a declining sector can be long and arduous, given the small number of job openings relative to growth industries, and recall provisions governing much of the unionized sector. And then, even if the search is successful, common seniority practices within manufacturing may work against the displaced worker. Come the next downturn or "restructuring," the displaced worker is likely to be right back out on the street.

While acknowledging the difficulties associated with this third option, it is too often overlooked in policy discussions on worker adjustment. What has become evident is that, for many workers, reemployment in a familiar setting stabilizes earnings levels. For the displaced worker with some job experience, the added difficulty of finding a familiar job may well be offset by the additional earnings from a comparable-wage job. As we shall see, many workers who would be considered vulnerable to earnings loss are instead making blue-collar transitions which avoid downward mobility, but still take relatively long periods of time to complete successfully.

In this chapter, we view these options as both policy alternatives and worker choices. Just as individuals must select a primary road to recovery, the federal government must also determine what it will help workers to achieve. Policymakers must come to grips with the implications of recent economic changes and the tradeoffs they pose for facilitating successful worker adjustment. Of the three options presented above, two would focus on helping workers obtain comparable-wage jobs, through either extended job search or education and skill upgrading. The third option would forego comparable wages in favor of a policy that emphasized rapid reemployment, preferably in a growth sector.

While reemployment in a comparable-wage job is, to many, the preferred option, it may not always be feasible. The program investments needed by many workers to overcome the education and training gaps they face may be too great to pursue in the current policy and spending context. And although programs can help workers simply search for comparable-wage jobs, the relatively long time it would take may be too much for society to endorse, or financially support. At the same time, the wage losses that often result from policies emphasizing rapid reemployment may also be unpalatable to both policymakers and unemployed workers themselves. Vexing as they may be, these issues define the challenges of worker displacement policy. As a result, it is quite important to consider carefully each policy option and the types of program investments that would be necessary to ensure their success.

Accordingly, we now turn to an assessment of the feasibility and appropriateness of these policy alternatives. We accomplish this by extending the analysis in the previous chapter to the recent postlayoff experience of displaced workers, paying particular attention to the use made by these workers of the above three options. The analysis relies on the Displaced Worker Supplement to the Current Population Survey (CPS) administered by the Bureau of Labor Statistics in January 1986. The CPS is a monthly survey of a random sample of approximately 60,000 U.S. households, and is most commonly known as the source for U.S. unemployment rate estimates.

The supplemental displacement data were gathered on all household members within the CPS aged 20 or older who lost or left a job in the five years preceding the survey because of a plant closing, permanent reduction in force, layoff without recall as of January 1986, or some similar reason. Those identified as displaced were asked a series of follow-up questions about their former job and the time since it was lost. The answers allow for a comparison of the current and former jobs by earnings level, occupation, and industry.

Our analysis sample includes 5,294 private, nonagricultural, wage-salary workers between the ages of 20 and 61 who lost or left a full-time job because of a plant closing, permanent reduction in force, or slack work between January 1981 and January 1986.[2] Unlike other studies, we have not excluded workers with limited tenure from the analysis. Such exclusions introduce statistical biases as a result of nonrandom sample selection, and potentially exclude a group of workers who may well have readjustment problems following layoff. Low tenure does not imply weak attachment to the labor force or to an occupation or industry. In many instances, low-tenure workers could have been laid off after accepting a particular job. In the face of "hired last-fired first" seniority provisions in many firms, these workers may find themselves going from one low-tenure job to another, especially in high unemployment areas. Like other displaced workers, they face the prospect of postlayoff readjustment problems.

The regular monthly CPS data is also used to make general comparisons between displaced workers, full-time growth-sector workers, and all full-time workers. The CPS also provides data which can be used to estimate the national wage distribution. A random one-fourth of all workers in the regular CPS report their weekly wages. This random sample is used to calculate the wage distribution of all full-time workers in January 1986, and to conduct comparisons between the displaced and the general population of full-time workers.

Patterns of Reemployment

By January 1986, the United States was in its fourth year of an economic expansion. For displaced workers, the ability to find reemployment and the number of weeks spent unemployed conform closely to general expectations about the difficulties facing manufacturing and blue-collar workers (table 3.2). Among all full-time workers displaced during the year immediately preceding the survey (i.e., losing jobs in 1985), only 40 percent had found full-time reemployment. Another 10 percent were working part time but, for the most part, desired a full-time job, while an additional 42 percent were recorded as unemployed. The remaining 9 percent opted out of the labor force altogether (although some were no doubt discouraged workers who had given up an active job search). While these reemployment rates are not high, they reflect the immediate postdisplacement experience. The experience of those displaced some time ago tell us more about the enduring impacts of job loss.

Workers displaced in 1984 (i.e., at least one full year before the survey) were more successful in finding new employment. By January 1986, 65 percent were reemployed full time and only 15.8 percent were unemployed. In fact, it seems that after a year or two, the experience of the displaced levels off at about 65 to 70 percent who become reemployed full time, 10 to 11 percent who find part-time work (half of whom desire full-time work), 8 to 9 percent who remain unemployed, and 11 to 13 percent who drop out of the labor force. In other words, two years following displacement, the conventional unemployment rate for the displaced (the unemployed as a fraction of the active

Table 3.2

Reemployment Rates and Total Weeks of Unemployment Since Lost Job[a] (Row percentages are shown)

	Total weeks of unemployment since lost job			Employment status as of January 1986				
	0–14	15–26	27+	Reemployed full time	Reemployed part time (voluntary)	Reemployed part time (involuntary)	Unemployed	Out of the labor force
All full-time displaced workers	53.2	16.3	30.5	59.3	3.7	6.2	20.2	10.6
Layoff Industry								
Manufacturing	44.5	17.9	37.5	59.0	2.8	5.2	21.1	11.8
Other goods-producing	59.2	14.5	26.2	60.0	2.2	6.5	23.9	7.2
Transport., Comm., Util.	59.3	14.5	26.2	60.0	2.2	6.5	23.9	7.2
Trade	61.4	14.8	23.8	60.3	4.7	5.9	17.4	11.6
FIRE	60.8	19.6	19.6	66.1	3.4	7.5	16.1	6.8
Other services	62.7	14.4	22.8	56.6	6.9	9.4	17.0	10.0
Layoff Occupation								
Executive, Prof., Mgt.	63.2	17.0	19.8	68.4	5.2	5.6	13.7	7.0
Technical	64.9	15.9	19.2	72.6	2.4	2.8	13.8	8.4
Sales	61.8	18.3	19.8	63.2	5.6	5.4	15.1	10.6
Admin. support and clerical	51.9	17.3	30.8	57.3	4.7	6.2	15.6	16.1
Service	58.2	15.2	26.6	49.4	6.5	9.0	18.0	17.0
Craft and repair	53.1	16.0	30.8	62.4	2.1	5.9	21.2	8.3
Semiskilled	45.4	15.5	39.0	53.7	2.8	6.6	25.5	11.2
Sex								
Male	56.1	16.1	27.8	64.8	2.1	5.6	21.7	6.0
Female	45.7	16.5	35.9	48.7	6.7	7.8	17.1	19.7
Education								
Less than high school graduate	43.4	15.2	41.3	42.8	2.7	7.4	29.0	18.0
High school graduate	52.5	16.2	31.2	59.2	3.6	6.4	20.2	10.4
1–3 years posthigh school	58.4	17.2	24.4	66.6	4.3	4.6	17.2	7.2
4 years+ posthigh school	62.7	16.6	20.6	74.3	4.4	5.6	10.4	5.2
Year of Displacement								
1981	43.1	14.9	42.0	70.8	3.4	6.6	8.4	10.6
1982	43.3	13.8	42.8	70.0	5.0	4.5	9.0	11.4
1983	47.8	15.6	36.5	66.6	5.0	6.1	9.4	12.8
1984	49.4	17.0	33.6	64.6	2.8	5.6	15.8	11.0
1985 or January 1986	69.4	18.4	12.2	39.6	2.6	7.4	41.7	8.7

a. Data from the January 1986 Current Population Survey. All data refer to individuals aged 20–61 in January 1986. Displaced workers lost or left a full-time, private, nonagricultural, wage-salary job between January 1981 and January 1986 because of a plant closing, permanent reduction in force, or slack work, without recall as of January 1986.

labor force) drops to about 9 to 11 percent, at a time when the national unemployment rate was hovering around 7 percent.

As would be expected, unemployment probabilities increase for workers from declining sectors, from blue-collar occupations, for the less educated, and to some extent for men. Among semiskilled, blue-collar workers, who constitute over one-third of the displacement population, 26 percent were unemployed at the time of the survey and 39 percent had more than half a year of unemployment after layoff. For those with less than a high school education the situation was worse; 29 percent were unemployed at the time of the survey and 41 percent had more than half a year of unemployment since layoff.

Optimistically, one might hope that the pattern of reemployment follows the growth sectors of the economy. This would facilitate flexible labor market adjustment and the ability of worker assistance programs to place individuals in jobs. Indeed, the experience of displaced workers indicates that many workers do find new jobs in growing sectors. Just over 60 percent of all reemployed workers found their job in a growth industry, and nearly 46 percent moved there from a slow growing or declining industry (table 3.3).

In addition, most reemployed job losers change occupation, industry, or both. The Bureau of the Census identifies 13 detailed occupational groupings (from "executive, administrative, and managerial" to "handlers and equipment cleaners") and 22 major industries (from "mining" to "hospitals"). Using these categories, only 23 percent of the reemployed remain in their old detailed industry and occupation; 44 percent change both industry and occupation, while another 12 percent change occupation while remaining in the old industry. On the surface, it seems that displacement is typically followed by substantial occupational and interindustry mobility.

A closer examination of the data reveals less fundamental mobility by occupation and industry. The job loser, while often changing his or her specific occupation or industry, tends to stay in the same general economic sector. On the whole, blue-collar workers are finding new, blue-collar jobs, and workers from declining industries are becoming reemployed in new jobs within those same industries. By this account, the labor market does not appear as flexible across sectors as it does

Table 3.3
Reemployment Mechanisms Among Dislocated Workers[a]

Reemployment job characteristics	All displaced workers	Layoff occupation			Layoff industry		Layoff job in a high-growth industry	
		Skilled blue-collar	Semiskilled	White-collar and service	Goods-producing	Service-producing	Yes	No
Skilled blue-collar	20.8	54.6	16.0	8.5	24.3	15.8	21.7	20.0
Semiskilled	23.1	20.4	46.6	6.9	29.6	13.7	14.6	30.4
White-collar and service	56.1	24.9	37.4	84.6	46.1	70.5	63.6	49.6
Goods-producing	41.9	58.1	50.4	28.1	56.6	20.8	30.5	51.8
Service-producing	58.1	41.9	49.6	71.9	43.4	79.2	69.5	48.2
High-growth sector	60.6	56.9	51.4	69.1	52.2	72.6	77.8	45.7
Slow-growth/declining sector	39.4	43.1	48.6	30.9	47.8	27.4	22.0	54.3
Changed major occupation/same industry[b]	12.4	13.2	12.6	11.9	13.4	11.1	10.7	14.0
Changed major industry/same occupation	20.5	23.7	11.5	25.7	19.4	22.2	21.6	19.6
Changed major industry and occupation	43.9	32.2	54.1	41.8	43.3	44.7	44.9	43.0
Same major industry and occupation	23.2	30.9	21.8	20.6	24.0	22.0	22.8	23.5
Moved to new city or county to take/look for a new job	17.6	19.2	15.3	18.8	18.4	16.4	18.1	17.2

a. Data from the January 1986 Current Population Survey. All data refer to individuals aged 20–61 in January 1986. Displaced workers lost or left a full-time, private, nonagricultural, wage-salary job between January 1981 and January 1986 because of a plant closing, permanent reduction in force, or slack work, without recall as of January 1986.

b. The 13 major occupations in the Current Population Survey include eight white-collar and service categories, "farm, forestry, and fisheries," craft and repair (skilled blue-collar), and three semiskilled blue-collar occupational categories.

within them. Following layoff, the majority of workers seem to end up in the same broad field in which they began. If policymakers wish to pursue a strategy of intersector mobility, they will have to overcome a strong behavioral link between displaced workers and the job opportunities they face.

For example, only 25 percent of skilled and 37 percent of semiskilled blue-collar workers moved into white-collar and service jobs, while the majority found new blue-collar employment. Moreover, 54 percent of workers from the declining and slow-growing industries found new jobs within these same industries (which include all of manufacturing plus transportation, communication, and public utilities).

Although semiskilled blue-collar workers are more likely to move into white-collar and service jobs than skilled workers, almost two-thirds remain in blue-collar positions, half become reemployed in traditional goods-producing industries, and about half find jobs in slow-growing and declining industries. Displaced white-collar and service workers often change industry and occupation, but the vast majority (85 percent) find new white-collar and service jobs, and almost 70 percent are reemployed in the high-growth sectors.

Why do blue-collar workers have such an obvious preference for blue-collar and declining sector jobs, despite the relative scarcity of such positions? Part of the answer lies in their qualifications for growing jobs and the risk of experiencing an earnings loss. To see this, we divided the January 1986 sample of all full-time workers into four quartiles of equal size. The low-wage quartile earned less than $237 per week, the low-middle $237–$350, the high-middle $351–$500, and the high-wage quartile more than $500 weekly.[3] We then compared the human capital attributes of displaced workers with those of other workers in each quartile. Our results show clearly that the displaced are not well matched to either the average job in the economy or those in growth sectors. As would be expected, these mismatches increase as one moves up the earnings ladder (table 3.4).

For example, while displaced workers are fairly well-represented in the upper two earnings quartiles on their old jobs, the vehicle through which they achieved this high-wage status is quite different from that

THE ROAD TO RECOVERY

Table 3.4
Selected Characteristics of Displaced Workers, All Full-Time Workers and Growth-Sector Workers, by Earnings Quartile[a,b]

Worker characteristics	Lowest quartile			Low-middle quartile			High-middle quartile			Highest quartile		
	Displaced workers	All full-time workers	Growth sector	Displaced workers	All full-time workers	Growth sector	Displaced workers	All full-time workers	Growth sector	Displaced workers	All full-time workers	Growth sector
N (000s)	2,367	14,880	10,715	2,185	15,609	9,817	1,780	14,677	7,936	1,690	13,831	6,663
Education												
<H.S. graduate	28.5	23.2	19.8	23.1	16.4	13.2	16.9	11.4	8.5	10.8	6.9	5.9
H.S. graduate	50.4	54.3	54.6	49.3	50.6	48.6	46.4	44.8	39.5	38.2	28.0	23.5
1–3 years post-H.S.	15.3	16.2	18.5	18.4	21.2	24.0	23.8	23.0	25.1	24.8	23.9	24.7
4 + years post-H.S.	5.8	6.3	7.1	9.3	11.8	14.2	12.8	20.8	26.9	26.2	41.2	45.9
Sex												
Male	42.7	34.9	32.7	66.1	50.3	47.7	76.4	67.0	58.8	87.7	84.8	79.7
Female	57.3	65.1	67.3	33.9	49.7	52.3	23.6	33.0	41.2	12.3	15.2	10.3
Occupation												
Exec., Prof., and Tech.	9.3	7.6	9.3	12.6	12.6	21.6	23.1	29.4	37.4	33.4	49.0	50.5
Sales	8.7	14.4	19.2	9.7	10.2	15.0	6.8	10.0	15.8	8.6	13.2	22.6
Admin. support & cler.	12.3	20.0	22.3	11.5	25.2	27.9	8.7	16.0	15.0	4.7	5.6	5.0
Service	11.8	22.8	30.9	5.0	7.6	10.8	1.7	3.9	5.9	1.6	0.8	0.6
Craft and repair	13.9	8.8	6.4	18.8	13.8	12.9	24.6	20.0	17.6	29.2	19.9	15.9
Semiskilled	44.0	26.4	11.8	40.3	25.7	11.8	37.2	20.6	8.2	22.5	12.6	5.4
Industry												
High-growth industries	48.6	72.0	100.0	44.7	62.8	100.0	40.9	54.1	100.0	43.1	48.2	100.0
Low-growth and stagnating	51.4	28.0	—	55.3	37.2	—	59.1	45.9	—	56.9	51.8	—

a. Data from the January 1986 Current Population Survey. All data refer to individuals aged 20–61 in January 1986. Displaced workers lost or left a full-time, private, nonagricultural wage-salary job between January 1981 and January 1986 because of a plant closing, permanent reduction in force, or slack work, without recall as of January 1986.

b. The earnings quartiles are based on the national full-time wage and salary distribution of all workers employed in January 1986. See page 70 for a description of the cutoffs.

for the average worker—and strikingly different from that of the growth-sector worker. Typically, the higher-wage worker is relatively well-educated, and productivity is clearly tied to his or her many years of schooling and professional training. In the highest earnings quartile in January 1986, for example, 41 percent of all workers had a four-year college degree, while only 35 percent had a high school degree or less. For growth-sector workers in the highest quartile, education is even more important: 46 percent have a four-year degree, and only 29 percent have a high school degree or less education.

In comparison, displaced workers in the highest-wage quartile have earned that position in large part through on-the-job skills, which are not directly related to formal educational achievement. Only 26 percent of the high-wage displaced have a four-year college degree, 11 percent never completed high school, and 38 percent are high school graduates. The educational gap reflects the occupational disparities between the displaced and the growth-sector workers. Over half of the high-wage displaced are blue-collar workers, while only one in five growth-sector jobs is blue-collar. Moreover, those blue-collar jobs that are available in growth sectors tend to be skilled positions, while many of the job-losers were in semiskilled jobs.

At lower wage levels, there are fewer disparities between the educational backgrounds of displaced workers, full-time workers, and growth-sector workers in general, but a small educational gap remains. Many low-wage workers are women in sales, administrative support, service, and unskilled manufacturing positions. Lower-wage occupations experiencing rapid employment growth are concentrated in the service and trading sectors. On average, employees in these low-wage jobs are slightly more educated than the displaced workers, many of whom are losing semiskilled blue-collar jobs. However, the educational gap is relatively small, and the prospects for maintaining wage levels would seem to be somewhat better for these lower-wage displaced than for their higher-wage counterparts.

These comparisons are consistent with the broad labor market trends discussed in the previous chapter. They suggest that many job-losers, particularly those from higher-wage blue-collar jobs, will qualify for few of the white-collar and service jobs at comparable-wage levels, while lower-wage workers will likely find job offers across a broader spectrum of less skilled occupations. While this helps to explain the limited number of workers who change industries and occupations, it also suggests that a short-term investment strategy, such as that adopted under JTPA, may be best suited for workers in the bottom half of the wage and salary distribution. Although these workers will often need educational upgrading and occupational training, the required investment is limited by the large number of other lower-wage opportunities for which they are more or less already qualified.

In stark contrast is the higher-wage, blue-collar worker. Compared to other high-wage workers, these individuals have significant education and training deficiencies. Absent substantial training investments, programs will have little else to offer many of them than simply a job, or assistance in finding one. While some will be lucky enough to return to their layoff field, for others, such assistance can often amount to accepting an earnings loss and some amount of de-skilling. As we have seen, workers have a clear interest in avoiding this, by virtue of their searching for opportunities in their old fields of employment.

Reemployment patterns by layoff wage confirm this result. Among high-wage, skilled, blue-collar workers finding new jobs, 80 percent remain in blue-collar occupations, and a full 40 percent are working in their old occupation and industry (table 3.5). Moving down the wage distribution, there is more mobility. In the lowest earnings quartile, over one-third of displaced skilled workers finding new jobs moved into white-collar and service occupations, and only 19 percent found jobs in their old major industry and occupation.

Further evidence of the likely reluctance of high-wage skilled workers to move into new types of jobs can be found in the data on geographic mobility. Among the skilled workers from the highest wage quartile, 27 percent of the reemployed moved to a new city or county in order to look for or accept a new job. This represents a relatively high rate of geographic mobility, over 10 percentage points greater than that for skilled workers in each of the three lower-wage quartiles. Clearly, the higher-wage workers may well be moving to avoid the earnings declines associated with movement into new occupations and

Table 3.5
Reemployment Mechanisms Among Dislocated Workers,
by Layoff Wage Quartile and Occupation[a]

Reemployment mechanisms	Former wage quartile[b]			
	Lowest	Low-middle	High-middle	Highest
Skilled workers (former job)				
Skilled blue-collar	36.2	54.5	55.6	63.9
Semiskilled	26.5	21.4	21.1	16.6
White-collar and service	37.3	24.1	23.3	19.5
Goods-producing	45.7	53.3	54.1	68.9
Service-producing	54.3	46.7	45.9	31.1
High-growth sector	63.2	61.4	54.7	56.0
Slow-growth/decline	36.8	38.6	45.3	44.0
Changed major occupation/same industry	20.7	7.6	14.4	11.7
Changed major industry/same occupation	17.1	27.2	27.6	23.5
Changed major industry and occupation	43.1	37.9	30.0	24.4
Same major industry and occupation	19.2	27.3	28.0	40.4
Moved to new city/county to accept/look for a new job	16.5	14.0	16.6	27.1
Semiskilled (former job)				
Skilled blue-collar	13.4	16.4	17.1	20.1
Semiskilled	40.5	45.8	50.6	51.7
White-collar and service	46.2	37.8	32.3	28.2
Goods-producing	48.2	50.4	51.4	55.6
Service-producing	51.8	49.6	48.6	44.4
High-growth sector	53.4	49.9	53.1	47.5
Slow-growth/decline	46.6	50.1	46.9	52.5
Changed major occupation/same industry	13.7	10.7	10.5	14.4
Changed major industry/same occupation	11.7	11.3	11.6	12.0
Changed major industry and occupation	56.8	57.5	52.8	48.0
Same major industry and occupation	17.8	20.5	25.1	25.6
Moved to new city/county to accept/look for a new job	13.2	17.3	15.0	18.3
White-collar and service (former job)				
Skilled blue-collar	5.6	9.2	9.9	8.9
Semiskilled	8.6	7.2	7.9	5.0
White-collar and service	85.8	83.6	82.3	86.1
Goods-producing	20.9	25.3	27.3	36.2
Service-producing	79.1	74.7	72.7	63.8
High-growth sector	75.0	71.3	68.4	63.0
Slow-growth/decline	25.0	28.7	31.6	37.0
Changed major occupation/same industry	11.5	10.8	16.0	10.6
Changed major industry/same occupation	23.3	24.9	26.4	29.2
Changed major industry and occupation	50.4	47.4	37.0	30.7
Same major industry and occupation	14.8	16.9	20.6	29.5
Moved to new city/county to accept/look for a new job	15.2	16.8	17.6	26.2

a. Data from the January 1986 Current Population Survey. All data refer to individuals aged 20–61 in January 1986. Displaced workers lost or left a full-time, private, nonagricultural, wage-salary job between January 1981 and January 1986 because of a plant closing, permanent reduction in force, or slack work, without recall as of January 1986.

b. The earnings quartiles are based on the national full-time wage and salary distribution of all workers employed in January 1986. See page 70 for a description of the cutoffs.

industries: 69 percent of the highest-wage skilled workers were reemployed in the goods-producing industries.

Semiskilled blue-collar workers are, in general, less likely to move into growth sectors than their skilled counterparts, no matter what their former earnings quartile (in some parts of the country there has been substantial growth in skilled construction jobs, which may account for the difference). Occupational mobility is more common among the semiskilled, but again varies according to the former wage quartile. The rate of mobility into white-collar and service occupations is 46 percent for the lowest-wage workers, but only 28 percent for the highest-wage workers. Like skilled workers, the semiskilled seem to be avoiding the transition into white-collar and service work, especially when displaced from higher-wage jobs.

Nevertheless, a surprising result from the CPS displaced worker survey is the overall degree of success enjoyed by many displaced workers in finding comparable-wage jobs. For example, of our sample of displaced full-time workers who were working for pay in January 1986, 40 percent had higher real earnings on the new job than on the lost job, while 32 percent saw their earnings reduced to less than three-fourths of the predisplacement level.

Typically, comparisons between layoff and reemployment earnings have followed this approach and analyzed earnings loss in percentage change terms.[4] This offers the advantage of simplicity and allows one to directly observe the magnitude of the loss (or gain) overall and on a subgroup basis. Here, however, we have chosen instead to assess the relative earnings position of displaced workers by analyzing their movement across each of the quartiles of the wage and salary distribution. While less precise in judging the size of any earnings change, this approach does allow one to determine how displacement has affected a key social indicator—one's standing in the earnings distribution. This makes judgments of earnings loss more intuitively appealing and also provides a bounded target rather than a particular level for defining a comparable-wage job. It does, however, have the disadvantage of potentially masking large, within-quartile changes, and like percentage changes, overstating any earnings loss for those workers

Table 3.6
Job Changing and Relative Earnings[a]

	All full-time displaced	Former wage quartile[b]			
		Lowest	Low-middle	High-middle	Highest
Number reemployed (000s)	5,061	1,324	1,372	1,211	1,153
January 1986 Wage Quartile					
Lowest	34.0	67.9	35.4	21.2	9.1
	(.66)	(.93)	(.63)	(.39)	(.26)
Low-middle	28.6	24.0	42.8	30.1	14.5
	(.95)	(1.43)	(1.00)	(.73)	(.43)
High-middle	20.8	7.0	16.9	33.3	27.0
	(1.01)	(2.07)	(1.40)	(1.01)	(.74)
Highest	16.7	1.1	4.9	15.3	49.4
	(1.11)	(3.98)	(1.83)	(1.48)	(1.01)

NOTE: Numbers in parentheses are median ratio between January 1986 weekly earnings and former earnings. Former earnings are inflated to January 1986 dollars using the CPI.

a. Data from the January 1986 Current Population Survey. All data refer to individuals aged 20–61 in January 1986. Displaced workers lost or left a full-time, private, nonagricultural, wage-salary job between January 1981 and January 1986 because of a plant closing, permanent reduction in force, or slack work, without recall as of January 1986.

b. The earnings quartiles are based on the national full-time wage and salary distribution of all workers employed in January 1986. See page 70 for a description of the cutoffs.

who, at the time of layoff, were at the lower bound of any one quartile.[5]

Overall, our results show that roughly two-thirds of reemployed displaced workers found jobs that allowed them to remain in their old wage quartile or move up (table 3.6). Workers from the higher-wage quartiles had the most difficulty maintaining their relative earnings, but even they were successful in doing so about half the time. For workers in the three higher-wage quartiles finding new jobs in their old quartiles, the median ratio of present to former earnings was 100 percent. In other words, most workers were able to maintain or improve their earnings position.

What this obscures, however, is the not unsubstantial fraction of displaced workers who suffer a severe drop in their earnings position. Among the highest-quartile workers, for example, 27 percent move into the high-middle quartile, 14 percent into the low-middle quartile, and 9 percent fall all the way down into the lowest quartile. The median ratios of present to former earnings as a result of this downward mobility are .74, .43, and .26, respectively. Over half of those losing jobs in the high-middle quartile are reemployed in the lower two quartiles, while 35 percent of those in the low-middle quartile move down into the lowest quartile. Therefore, while many displaced workers are successful in finding comparable-wage reemployment, hundreds of thousands experience downward mobility in both an absolute and relative sense.

Given the emphasis in other research upon percentage earnings changes following job loss, we also assessed the relationship between these changes and movements within and across the earnings distribution. Two findings, in particular, are worth noting. The first is that large percentage reductions in earnings (e.g., greater than 25 percent) rarely leave a worker in the same quartile. Regardless of one's status at the time of layoff, percentage reductions in excess of 25 percent are never experienced by more than 32 percent of those maintaining their status in the distribution; as would be expected, this percentage share declines rapidly as one moves down the distribution. Overall, those workers whose earnings drop by more than 25 percent typically also drop down the distribution by at least one quartile.

Second, there is some evidence that movements down the distribution may be influenced by relatively small percentage reductions among workers whose layoff earnings were at or near the lower bound of a quartile. However, this occurrence was generally limited to those experiencing percentage losses of less than 25 percent and was most evident among higher-wage workers. Take, for example, workers who began in the highest quartile of the distribution (weekly earnings in excess of $500) and became reemployed in the second highest quartile of the wage and salary distribution. Among these workers, 47 percent experienced a percentage earnings decline of no more than 25 percent, suggesting that their layoff earnings were likely close to the lower cutoff of the quartile. In contrast, among workers beginning in the next to lowest quartile and becoming reemployed in the lowest quartile of the distribution, only 26 percent experienced a percentage reduction of less than 25 percent. For these workers, 48 percent experienced a 50 to 74 percent earnings reduction, while the remainder had reemployment earnings that were less than half of those on the layoff job.

On balance, these results suggest that within-quartile movements are rarely associated with large percentage wage reductions, and that relatively small losses of less than 25 percent do not usually result in movements down the wage and salary distribution. The findings also indicate that the focus of prior studies on percentage losses in excess of 25 percent may well be an appropriate cutoff to signal the need for concern and assistance. In addition to its magnitude per se, earnings losses of this size are usually sufficient to drop a worker down at least one quartile in the wage and salary distribution.

A good deal of the downward mobility which does occur seems to follow from the human capital gaps that many displaced workers face. These gaps increase substantially as one moves up the earnings ladder and appear to limit the types of changes that workers are either willing or able to make. Those faced with no alternative but to change fields of work are most at risk to earnings loss. As a result, programs and policies to assist these workers must either help them obtain comparable jobs or counsel them to enter a new line of work. As is becoming evident, either can be a difficult task.

Relative Human Capital and Earnings

It is useful to analyze the reemployment wage patterns of displaced workers as resulting from the transferability (or lack thereof) of human capital across comparable-wage jobs. While displaced-worker programs are attuned to the notion of improving human capital, not enough attention has been paid to the scope of the investment needed to facilitate a successful readjustment. We have seen that some displaced workers are particularly at risk today because they lack human capital relative to workers in growth sectors of the economy, and most especially relative to those earning wages comparable to that which the job loser is accustomed. Further, the gap in human capital is as much in general education as it is in specific vocational skills. For workers under family pressure to find comparable-wage employment, the gap can seem insurmountable. It is a worker's relative human capital—i.e.

his or her mix of skills and abilities relative to those workers in the same earnings class—which is most likely to determine the degree of earnings replacement on the new job.

If we follow the earnings outcome of displaced workers in the higher-wage quartiles, the importance of human capital transferability becomes quite evident (table 3.7). Beginning with workers displaced from the highest wage and salary quartile, recall that, overall, 49 percent of the reemployed remained in the highest quartile. However, in the current labor market environment, general education and other "growth-sector skills" appear to be much more valuable than experience in a blue-collar setting. As a result, a full 69 percent of reemployed executive, professional, and managerial workers were able to remain in the highest-wage quartile, as did 52 percent of technical workers. Sales workers, clericals, and service workers had relatively little success maintaining high-wage positions; however, few of these workers had high-wage jobs to begin with.

Among skilled blue-collar workers from the highest-wage quartile, the situation was not as favorable. Less than 50 percent of the reemployed found new, high-wage jobs, while 20 percent dropped to the lower half of the wage distribution.[6] For the semiskilled, the situation is even worse. Once reemployed, these high-wage workers spread out almost evenly throughout the wage distribution. One-fifth end up in the lowest-earnings quartile, 23 percent become reemployed in the low-middle quartile, and only 29 percent are able to maintain their relative earnings position. Among displaced workers from the high-middle quartile, the situation is similar: skilled blue-collar workers, on average, drop their earnings position to some extent, while the semiskilled take it on the chin.

The relative human capital gap in general education for high-wage displaced workers also affects their reemployment earnings. Among those with less than a high school education, only 21 percent of the highest-wage workers and 31 percent of high-middle wage workers are able to maintain (or improve) their earnings position. High school graduates have somewhat better success in finding comparable-wage jobs (40 percent for the highest-wage quartile, 43 percent for the high-middle quartile). But these success rates pale against those for

Table 3.7
Relative Earnings of Reemployed Displaced Workers by Wage Quartile[a,b]
(Row percentages are shown)

| | High-middle quartile on former job | | | | Highest-quartile on former job | | | |
| | Reemployment earnings quartile | | | | Reemployment earnings quartile | | | |
	Lowest	Low-middle	High-middle	Highest	Lowest	Low-middle	High-middle	Highest
All Displaced	21.2	30.1	33.3	15.3	9.1	14.5	27.0	49.4
Education								
Less than high school graduate	33.2	35.5	24.2	7.2	22.6	26.0	30.2	21.2
High school graduate	21.7	35.2	32.4	10.7	11.2	18.7	29.7	40.4
1–3 years post-high school	16.4	23.4	39.4	20.7	9.1	12.9	30.2	47.7
4-year college graduate	15.5	19.8	35.6	29.1	2.5	7.2	19.4	70.8
Layoff Occupation								
Executive and professional	15.9	21.5	36.3	26.3	2.7	9.2	18.6	69.4
Technical	10.2	22.8	43.8	23.2	1.1	19.3	27.2	52.4
Sales	12.8	32.6	34.2	20.4	4.6	16.5	40.0	38.9
Admin. support and clerical	11.2	34.0	43.6	11.2	21.0	12.4	28.0	38.6
Service	7.8	50.2	26.8	15.3	24.6	13.1	37.2	25.1
Skilled blue-collar	19.0	32.4	34.0	14.6	7.7	13.4	31.0	47.9
Semiskilled	31.7	31.3	27.5	9.5	20.1	22.8	28.1	29.0

a. Data from the January 1986 Current Population Survey. All data refer to individuals aged 20–61 in January 1986. Displaced workers lost or left a full-time, private, nonagricultural wage-salary job between January 1981 and January 1986 because of a plant closing, permanent reduction in force, or slack work, without recall as of January 1986.

b. The earnings quartiles are based on the national full-time wage and salary distribution of all workers employed in January 1986. See page 70 for a description of the cutoffs.

4-year college graduates (71 percent of highest-wage college grads find comparable-wage jobs, as do 66 percent of high-middle wage workers). Clearly, educated and highly skilled workers are better able to maintain their productivity, and therefore their wage levels, when displaced from jobs.

These results imply that the reemployment pattern which generates the most downward mobility is likely to be movement into new occupations and industries. To test this generally, we compared the earnings of displaced workers who became reemployed in new occupational areas with those of other employed workers, controlling for differences in human capital and personal characteristics.[7] Our findings revealed that the reemployment earnings of these workers were, on average, 23 percent less than other similar workers, and approximately 15 percent less than displaced workers who found jobs in a similar occupational field. It thus appears that changes in one's occupational field can indeed have an adverse effect on reemployment earnings.

This result is also evident on a subgroup basis and particularly among higher-wage and blue-collar workers (table 3.8). Among reemployed, skilled, blue-collar workers from the highest-wage quartile who changed both their major industry and occupation, two-thirds experienced downward mobility, and over 40 percent actually moved down into the bottom half of the wage distribution. Only 41 percent of those reemployed in white-collar and service jobs remained in the highest-wage quartile, as compared to 56 percent of workers finding new, skilled, blue-collar jobs.

The risks for high-wage semiskilled workers of changing occupation and industry are also substantial; nearly 85 percent of these workers experienced downward wage mobility. In comparison, almost half of those reemployed in their old industry and occupation remain in the highest-wage quartile. For the semiskilled, the movement into white-collar and service work is a recipe for wage reduction: 32 percent end up in the lowest quartile, another 23 percent in the low-middle quartile.

Why are the less educated and semiskilled workers so greatly affected by the displacement process? The answer is not simply that "good jobs" are being replaced by "bad jobs." If this was true we

Table 3.8
High-Wage Displaced Workers: Patterns of Earnings Change[a]
(Row percentages are shown)

Reemployment job characteristics for high-wage workers	Earnings quartile on reemployment job[b]			
	Lowest	Low-middle	High-middle	Highest
Skilled Blue-Collar (former job)				
Skilled blue-collar	7.4	4.7	31.9	56.0
Semiskilled	8.3	38.0	28.8	25.0
White-collar and service	8.3	20.2	30.0	41.4
Changed major occupation/same industry	0.0	22.6	45.0	32.5
Changed major industry/same occupation	18.5	9.9	35.7	36.0
Changed major industry and occupation	12.1	32.0	22.3	33.6
Same major industry and occupation	1.3	1.9	29.8	66.9
Semiskilled (former job)				
Skilled blue-collar	7.2	24.8	36.8	31.2
Semiskilled	18.8	22.0	25.5	33.7
White-collar and service	31.9	22.9	26.9	18.3
Changed major occupation/same industry	8.2	27.1	20.8	43.9
Changed major industry/same occupation	19.4	25.8	35.8	19.1
Changed major industry and occupation	29.6	25.3	29.0	16.1
Same major industry and occupation	10.8	14.6	27.3	47.4
White-Collar and Service (former job)				
Skilled blue-collar	10.9	14.4	21.9	52.8
Semiskilled	20.4	9.7	37.6	32.3
White-collar and service	4.1	11.6	23.9	60.4
Changed major occupation/same industry	4.8	10.9	32.5	51.8
Changed major industry/same occupation	2.3	13.4	21.9	62.3
Changed major industry and occupation	16.5	19.7	19.5	49.3
Same major industry and occupation	2.8	3.2	28.3	65.8

a. Data from the January 1986 Current Population Survey. All data refer to individuals aged 20–61 in January 1986. Displaced workers lost or left a full-time, private, nonagricultural, wage-salary job between January 1981 and January 1986 because of a plant closing, permanent reduction in force, or slack work, without recall as of January 1986.

b. The earnings quartiles are based on the national full-time wage and salary distribution of all workers employed in January 1986. See page 70 for a description of the cutoffs.

would expect all of the displaced to suffer proportionately. In fact, as discussed in the previous chapter, the service economy is creating ample shares of both good and bad jobs, but the good jobs being created in growth sectors today are concentrated in white-collar work to a degree that they were not previously. The economy is trading decent blue-collar jobs for a range of service sector ones. It is the education and training gap between the high-wage, less educated displaced and their comparable-wage, growth-sector counterparts that is creating difficulties for job-losers.

It is true that the displaced skilled and semiskilled worker can readily move into growth sectors—but more often than not as a health aide, a fast-food worker, or possibly a sales clerk or typist. The comparable-wage jobs that are available in growth sectors are mostly reserved for college graduates and those with years of prior service in the emergent industries. This situation creates a challenge for employment and training policy, which must find a way to fit the worker into the available supply of job vacancies.

As we have seen, this challenge revolves around the prior earnings and experience of displaced workers and whether the policy emphasis is on reemployment per se, or reemployment in a comparable-wage job. The feasibility or reemployment at comparable wages seems to be limited by the large human capital gaps between displaced and other workers, especially at the upper ends of the wage and salary distribution. In these cases, one cannot help but wonder if the required program investments are practical social objectives and program strategies. Part of the answer to this dilemma depends on the region in which workers reside, since most displaced workers search for new jobs in their initial areas of residence.

Displacement and Region

It is not only the human capital characteristics of less educated and semiskilled workers per se that place them at risk following displacement. It is also the fit between the job-loser and the skill mix in a particular local labor market that is important. Two factors on the demand side of the labor market are of primary importance: (1) the overall degree of economic expansion, which, together with attrition, will determine the number of job openings and the rate of wage growth; and (2) the differences between the skill requirements, educational requirements, and wage opportunities in expanding and declining sectors. Overall growth rates will influence the length of job search for the displaced, and will, in combination with the human capital "match" between job-losers and growth-sector workers, affect the earnings position of the displaced following layoff.

Variations in the economic performance of different regions of the U.S. provide a basis for assessing further the relationship between

economic growth, relative human capital, and postdisplacement outcomes. As discussed in the last chapter, regions have varied substantially with respect to both their overall rate of expansion and the types
of jobs being eliminated and created. By comparing the experiences of
displaced workers across regions, we can better judge the importance
of these varying demand-side factors upon the adjustment process.

To explore the impact of regional economic conditions on displaced
workers, we selected five of the census regions for further study: New
England (Maine, New Hampshire, Vermont, Massachusetts, Rhode
Island, Connecticut); Mid-Atlantic (New York, New Jersey, and Pennsylvania); East North Central (Ohio, Indiana, Illinois, Michigan, Wisconsin); South Atlantic (Delaware, Maryland, D.C., Virginia, West
Virginia, North and South Carolina, Georgia, and Florida); and West
South Central (Arkansas, Louisiana, Oklahoma, and Texas). Each of
these regions had large numbers of displaced workers as reported in the
January 1986 survey, but varied greatly in terms of overall economic
conditions and patterns of employment growth and decline (table 3.9).

Like that for the U.S., the picture that emerges from the reemployment patterns in the various regions is one of relative industrial and
occupational immobility, even in those areas where overall economic
conditions have been favorable (table 3.10). Overall, large proportions
of workers from all regions became reemployed in their layoff industry
and occupation as well as in goods-producing, declining, and slow-
growing sectors. In the East North Central states, for example, 48
percent of reemployed workers found jobs in goods-production and 42
percent were reemployed in slow-growing or declining industries. This
relative immobility occurred despite the precipitous decline of the
goods-producing sector in that region, and in contrast to the national
averages (42 percent and 39 percent, respectively).

In New England, with more favorable economic conditions, workers
also tended to remain in their old lines of work. Only 37 percent of
reemployed job-losers changed both their industry and occupation,
compared to a national average of 44 percent. In the other relatively
healthy divisions (the Mid-Atlantic and South Atlantic) the rates of
industry and occupational job changing were also at or slightly below
the average. However, in the West South Central region, a full 50

Table 3.9
Economic Indicators by Census Division, 1979–1985

Economic Indicators	U.S.	New England	Mid-Atlantic	East North Central	West North Central	South Atlantic	East South Central	West South Central	Mountain	Pacific
Unemployment rate, 1985[a]	7.2	4.4	6.8	8.8	6.2	6.1	9.0	7.9	6.8	7.4
Real personal income growth, 1979–1985[b]										
In total	16.4	24.2	15.6	4.0	12.3	25.5	11.1	23.1	21.8	18.8
Per capita	9.6	21.1	14.6	3.9	9.3	14.1	7.0	8.5	6.0	6.4
Employment change, 1979–85[c]										
Total	16.1	10.2	9.4	3.8	5.4	26.9	13.7	28.0	29.0	19.9
By sector:										
Durable goods	−7.6	−5.9	−22.1	−19.4	−13.3	16.4	−4.8	−3.4	25.0	9.6
Nondurable goods	−5.0	−16.2	−12.1	−13.9	−3.6	5.1	7.8	−10.7	12.2	3.5
Other goods-producing	35.8	38.2	26.9	0.1	−6.5	35.0	2.2	30.3	18.8	29.9
Trans., comm., util.	14.1	51.7	6.9	6.8	−4.6	22.7	−1.9	28.7	29.4	14.0
Trade	19.2	15.2	11.2	10.6	9.4	26.2	32.3	36.4	30.2	17.9
FIRE	26.4	39.8	21.7	22.3	29.5	26.9	6.8	40.7	29.7	25.4
Other services	34.2	14.4	36.7	31.3	17.8	45.6	26.1	51.8	38.3	32.8
Divisional weekly earnings quartiles, full-time Workers, January 1986 ($)[d]										
Lowest-quartile	<236	<250	<250	<240	<209	<210	<190	<230	<230	<260
Low-middle quartile	236–349	250–358	250–364	240–363	209–311	210–299	190–278	230–349	230–334	260–399
High-middle quartile	350–500	359–500	365–505	364–520	312–461	300–475	279–400	350–500	335–500	400–575
Highest-quartile	>500	>500	>505	>520	>461	>475	>400	>500	>500	>575
Median full-time weekly earnings, January 1986 ($)[d]	350	360	365	364	312	300	280	350	336	400

a. *Employment and Earnings*, Bureau of Labor Statistics, U.S. Department of Labor.
b. *Survey of Current Business*, U.S. Department of Commerce, April 1986.
c. Data refer to wage and salary workers aged 16 to 61, employed in private, nonagricultural jobs. Estimates calculated by authors, based on March Supplements to the Current Population Survey.
d. Data from the January 1986 Current Population Survey. All data refer to individuals aged 20–61 in January 1986.

Table 3.10
Reemployment Mechanisms by Selected Census Divisions,
January 1986[a]

	Census division of residence, January 1986				
Reemployment mechanisms characteristics of new job	New England	Mid- Atlantic	East North Central	South Atlantic	West South Central
All Reemployed					
Skilled blue-collar	19.1	15.9	21.1	23.0	18.0
Semiskilled	25.3	23.5	25.3	24.8	23.3
White-collar and service	55.6	60.6	53.5	52.2	58.7
Goods-producing	49.1	42.2	47.8	40.7	36.6
Service-producing	50.9	57.8	52.2	59.3	63.4
Divisional high growth sector	61.5	63.2	58.0	47.2	79.0
Divisional slow growth/declining	38.5	36.8	42.0	52.8	21.0
Changed major occupation/same industry	14.2	12.8	15.5	12.6	9.7
Changed major industry/same occupation	19.7	20.9	17.0	23.2	21.6
Changed major industry and occupation	37.2	41.8	43.7	42.1	49.8
Same major industry and occupation	28.8	24.5	23.8	22.1	18.8
Moved to new city/county to accept/look for new job	15.6	13.1	14.6	17.2	20.5
Skilled Blue-Collar (former job)					
Skilled blue-collar	57.8	60.0	48.8	59.6	42.7
Semiskilled	18.7	22.8	25.5	16.4	27.8
White-collar and service	23.5	17.3	25.7	24.0	29.5
Goods-producing	62.1	61.2	63.0	58.0	54.9
Service-producing	37.9	38.8	37.0	42.0	45.1
Divisional high growth sector	60.8	61.7	42.8	56.5	68.4
Divisional slow growth/declining	39.2	38.3	57.2	43.5	31.6
Changed major occupation/same industry	7.7	10.6	16.9	12.7	13.0
Changed major industry/same occupation	13.7	23.8	18.9	29.0	24.8
Changed major industry and occupation	34.5	29.6	34.3	27.6	44.3
Same major industry and occupation	44.1	36.1	29.9	30.6	17.9
Moved to new city/county to accept/look for new job	7.6	16.1	15.3	17.1	20.8
Semiskilled Blue-Collar (former job)					
Skilled blue-collar	22.9	10.6	18.2	15.8	12.5
Semiskilled	54.0	47.4	43.4	48.5	46.6
White-collar and service	23.1	42.1	38.3	35.7	40.9
Goods-producing	64.0	54.2	53.8	47.9	41.5
Service-producing	36.0	45.8	46.2	52.1	58.3
Divisional high growth sector	45.7	52.2	50.2	38.9	75.9
Divisional slow growth/declining	54.3	47.8	49.8	61.1	24.1
Changed major occupation/same industry	15.7	14.6	16.0	11.3	7.0
Changed major industry/same occupation	10.1	10.1	9.2	12.5	11.2
Changed major industry and occupation	40.9	52.9	51.2	55.5	60.9
Same major industry and occupation	33.3	22.4	23.6	20.7	20.9
Moved to new city/county to accept/look for new job	8.2	10.6	14.0	16.1	19.4
White-Collar and Service (former job)					
Skilled blue-collar	3.9	5.4	10.4	8.8	9.9
Semiskilled	7.6	5.1	8.0	8.1	5.4

Table 3.10 continued
Reemployment Mechanisms by Selected Census Divisions,
January 1986[a]

Reemployment mechanisms characteristics of new job	Census division of residence, January 1986				
	New England	Mid-Atlantic	East North Central	South Atlantic	West South Central
White-collar and service	88.5	83.5	81.6	83.1	84.6
Goods-producing	34.4	26.6	34.7	24.3	24.6
Service-producing	65.6	73.4	65.3	75.7	75.4
Divisional high growth sector	72.4	72.2	71.5	49.5	85.9
Divisional slow growth/declining	27.6	27.8	28.5	50.5	14.1
Changed major occupation/same industry	15.3	12.1	14.3	13.8	9.9
Changed major industry/same occupation	28.3	28.3	23.4	29.4	27.1
Changed major industry and occupation	35.6	37.2	41.2	38.3	45.0
Same industry and occupation	20.8	22.4	21.1	18.5	18.0
Moved to new city/county to accept/look for new job	24.3	14.6	15.0	18.4	21.1

a. Data from the January 1986 Current Population Survey. All data refer to individuals aged 20–61 in January 1986. Displaced workers lost or left a full-time, private, nonagricultural, wage-salary job between January 1981 and January 1986 because of a plant closing, permanent reduction in force, or slack work, without recall as of January 1986.

percent of the reemployed changed both major industry and occupation.

Among skilled blue-collar workers, there was also a strong tendency to remain in a similar job and industry sector, despite variations in reemployment rates. Nationally, 62 percent of displaced skilled workers were reemployed full time as of January 1986, but in booming New England and the South Atlantic, and in the moderately healthy West South Central, the reemployment rates for skilled workers were 74 percent, 67 percent, and 67 percent, respectively.[8] In the East North Central, only 55 percent of displaced skilled workers had found new full-time jobs.

However, in each region, no less than 43 percent of skilled blue-collar workers became reemployed in similar jobs, and no more than 44 percent changed industry and occupation. In the relatively healthy New England, Mid-Atlantic, and South Atlantic regions, for example, 58 to 60 percent of the reemployed skilled workers found new, skilled blue-collar jobs, while the rest moved into semiskilled, white-collar, and service positions. In the other two (more economically distressed) regions, only about 45 percent of the skilled workers were reemployed in skilled jobs, with about half of the rest moving down into semi-skilled blue-collar jobs.

Semiskilled workers were reemployed full time at above-average rates in New England (60 percent), the South Atlantic (58 percent), and the West South Central (59 percent), but struggled in the Mid-Atlantic (47 percent) and the East North Central (52 percent). In four out of the five divisions, however, the reemployed either remained largely semiskilled workers (43 to 48 percent), or moved into white-collar and service jobs (36 to 42 percent). However, in New England the boom in construction trades and in services allowed most of the displaced to either remain in semiskilled employment (54 percent) or move up into skilled positions (23 percent).

Among white-collar and service workers, regional economic conditions had less of an impact. Since the number of jobs in these occupations was expanding in all regions, reemployment rates were high, most of the displaced found new white-collar and service jobs, and most were reemployed in the high-growth sectors in their divisions. In the divisions that have been creating many white-collar jobs recently (New England, the South Atlantic, the West South Central), 18 to 24 percent of the reemployed white-collar and service workers reported that they had "moved to a different city or county to look for work or to take a different job." It is likely that these high percentages of movers reflect the in-migration of white-collar workers from economically struggling regions.

To further assess the relationship between regional economic conditions and worker readjustment, we grouped states according to their unemployment rate relative to the national average, and then compared unemployment durations, reemployment rates, and various mobility measures. The results revealed several important findings (tables 3.11 and 3.12). First, it is clear that the likelihood and speed of reemployment is greater in low unemployment areas than in those areas experiencing above average rates of joblessness. This generally holds across industry, occupation, education, age, and sex groups, although blue-collar workers and the less educated do appear to be more sensitive to local economic conditions than their counterparts.

Second, almost regardless of local unemployment conditions, work-

Table 3.11
Reemployment and Total Weeks of Unemployment Since Lost Job,
by 1985 State Unemployment Rate[a]

	27+ weeks of unemployment since lost job			Reemployed full time, January 1986		
	States with high unem-ployment	States with average unem-ployment	States with low unem-ployment	States with high unem-ployment	States with average unem-ployment	States with low unem-ployment
All Full-Time Displaced	38.5	28.1	24.4	54.7	60.8	62.6
Layoff Industry						
Manufacturing	44.1	36.8	28.7	56.3	59.6	61.6
Other goods-producing	35.9	20.0	26.7	47.6	65.5	67.6
Trans., comm., util.	34.7	22.9	22.4	54.6	67.2	56.9
Trade	31.3	22.9	14.3	59.6	69.5	65.9
FIRE	27.0	16.6	19.6	71.6	63.3	67.7
Other services	32.7	18.6	20.4	49.8	58.1	62.4
Layoff Occupation						
Exec., prof., and mgr.	26.6	17.0	19.3	67.2	69.3	67.4
Technical	30.8	18.0	6.3	60.1	74.8	81.8
Sales	21.9	20.1	16.6	59.4	63.9	66.0
Admin. supp./clerical	49.8	23.6	27.8	60.4	56.4	56.1
Service	35.2	23.8	19.5	39.7	53.4	55.3
Craft and repair	38.7	28.6	22.9	51.8	65.4	73.0
Semiskilled	44.1	38.9	30.7	52.2	53.8	56.2
Education						
Less than H.S. graduate	51.7	39.2	30.5	37.9	42.9	50.6
H.S. graduate	38.0	29.1	25.1	52.8	62.0	62.7
1–3 years post-H.S.	32.6	22.6	17.0	65.3	66.9	67.5
4+ years post-H.S.	25.8	17.6	22.9	77.4	73.2	73.8
Sex						
Male	36.2	24.9	20.9	60.0	65.9	70.2
Female	43.9	34.2	30.2	42.1	51.2	50.1
Age						
20–24	25.4	17.4	14.4	43.0	55.6	54.3
25–34	34.9	25.2	22.6	59.1	63.0	65.0
35–44	42.6	31.0	26.2	59.4	65.9	70.9
45–54	43.9	33.3	27.9	53.3	58.5	56.0
55–61	55.4	46.3	37.6	41.5	44.0	53.9

a. Data from the January 1986 Current Population Survey. All data refer to individuals aged 20–61 in January 1986. Displaced workers lost or left a full-time, private, nonagricultural, wage-salary job between January 1981 and January 1986 because of a plant closing, permanent reduction in force, or slack work, without recall as of January 1986.

ers do appear to remain in the types of jobs and sectors from which they were laid off. While there is some evidence that mobility is inversely related to local unemployment rates, the relationship is not pronounced

Table 3.12
Reemployment Mechanisms, by 1985 State Unemployment Rate[a]

Reemployment mechanisms characteristics of new job	States with high unemployment	States with average unemployment	States with low unemployment
All Reemployed			
Skilled blue-collar	25.6	21.6	23.6
Semiskilled	21.7	20.3	20.9
White-collar and service	52.7	58.1	55.1
Changed major occupation/same industry	13.3	12.0	12.3
Changed major industry/same occupation	20.4	21.1	19.0
Changed major industry and occupation	43.5	43.2	46.4
Same major industry and occupation	22.8	23.7	22.2
Skilled Blue-Collar (former job)			
Skilled blue-collar	56.7	53.5	55.2
Semiskilled	16.8	22.5	19.3
White-collar and service	26.5	24.0	25.6
Changed major occupation/same industry	14.4	13.9	9.1
Changed major industry/same occupation	27.4	22.1	23.7
Changed major industry and occupation	28.9	32.6	35.8
Same major industry and occupation	29.3	31.4	31.4
Semiskilled Blue-Collar (former job)			
Skilled blue-collar	15.8	15.5	17.3
Semiskilled	49.1	45.0	46.9
White-collar and service	35.1	39.5	35.8
Changed major occupation/same industry	14.0	11.6	13.0
Changed major industry/same occupation	13.2	10.9	10.2
Changed major industry and occupation	50.7	56.9	52.5
Same major industry and occupation	22.1	20.6	24.3
White-Collar and Service (former job)			
Skilled blue-collar	9.8	7.9	8.7
Semiskilled	7.6	6.4	7.8
White-collar and service	82.6	85.8	83.6
Changed major occupation/same industry	12.1	11.9	13.2
Changed major industry/same occupation	23.8	27.1	23.8
Changed major industry and occupation	43.9	39.3	46.3
Same major industry and occupation	20.1	22.1	16.7

a. Data from the January 1986 Current Population Survey. All data refer to individuals aged 20–61 in January 1986. Displaced workers lost or left a full-time, private, nonagricultural, wage-salary job between January 1981 and January 1986 because of a plant closing, permanent reduction in force, or slack work, without recall as of January 1986.

and does not detract from the observed preference of workers to search for similar jobs.

If one approached this regional analysis with the hope that healthy areas could serve the twin goals of rapid reemployment and the movement of workers into new and growing industries and occupations, then the findings are less than fully satisfying. While reemployment rates are indeed higher in the rapidly growing areas, the findings show that blue-collar job-losers are more likely to move into growth sectors, to change industries, and to find new occupations in those areas where economic conditions are relatively poor.

Why is there not more movement of the displaced across occupations and industries in booming New England and in the high-growth South Atlantic? After all, it would seem that these areas would be most likely to have skill shortages in high-growth fields. Part of the answer, in all probability, has to do with the fact that those regions which have experienced the most rapid growth in service-producing sectors, the lowest unemployment rates, and the greatest overall economic expansion have, for the most part, had the smallest declines in their goods-producing employment.[9] For example, durable goods employment declined between 1979 and 1985 by only 6 percent in New England and 3 percent in the West South Central, while it increased by 16 percent in the South Atlantic. Displaced workers in these regions were no doubt faced with many more openings in durable goods manufacturing than were workers in the East North Central. Further, a slower rate of job decline in the healthy regions results in a smaller pool of displaced workers to begin with. Thus, those who do find themselves without jobs have less competition for the (larger) number of job openings.

As discussed earlier, the movement of workers back to their old industries and occupations is likely also a result of their inability to qualify for new, comparable-wage jobs. On a national basis, it was shown that obtaining such jobs was particularly difficult for high-wage workers holding blue-collar jobs in general, and skilled jobs in particular. Since some regions of the country have experienced more substantial change in their job structure than others, we examined this issue on a regional basis by comparing the characteristics of high-wage displaced workers with those of high-wage growth-sector workers.

Overall, our results confirm the national findings and also reveal that in some regions, the prospect of reemployment in a comparable-wage job is exceedingly difficult (table 3.13). For one thing, there are sharp differences between the characteristics of high-wage displaced workers and those employed in growth sectors. Across each of the five regions, growth-sector workers tend to be younger, better educated, and more

Table 3.13
Characteristics of Workers in the Highest Divisional Earnings Quartile, by Selected Census Divisions[a]

	New England		Mid-Atlantic		East North Central		South Atlantic		West South Central	
	Displaced workers	Growth sectors	Displaced workers	Growth sectors	Displaced workers	Growth sectors	Displaced workers	Growth sectors	Displaced workers	Growth sectors
N (000s)	57	552	201	1,195	297	978	197	959	281	1,099
Age										
20–24	1.3	2.0	1.7	6.4	1.7	3.6	2.4	6.7	1.8	1.4
25–34	32.6	28.5	31.2	39.9	31.0	30.7	27.8	29.8	39.9	38.2
35–44	24.7	37.3	30.1	25.2	38.6	41.5	35.4	30.5	31.1	35.4
45–54	23.6	23.2	22.8	19.9	27.6	16.6	27.4	25.0	19.5	20.8
55–61	17.8	9.0	14.1	8.7	21.8	7.6	7.0	8.0	8.7	4.1
Education										
Less than high school graduate	11.1	4.1	12.3	4.7	10.6	4.8	13.3	7.2	11.4	8.3
High school graduate	30.4	22.8	37.4	26.8	43.7	28.6	42.8	22.8	32.1	21.4
1–3 years post-high school	18.4	18.0	20.1	16.9	25.3	19.9	17.4	16.5	27.5	27.2
4 + years post-high school	40.1	55.1	30.3	51.6	20.4	46.8	26.5	53.6	29.1	43.1
Occupation										
Executive and professional	42.5	48.7	26.1	46.7	21.1	46.6	28.6	56.3	30.8	36.6
Technical and related	0.0	1.3	5.2	7.2	2.5	2.7	3.8	3.7	8.4	3.7
Sales	12.1	17.0	7.0	21.6	7.6	18.3	11.8	10.8	11.8	22.4
Admin. support and clerical	4.7	7.7	4.3	6.8	5.7	7.9	6.0	9.8	3.3	5.5
Service	0.0	1.7	5.3	0.5	1.1	1.2	0.0	1.7	0.0	0.0
Craft and repair	27.1	18.4	23.2	13.9	37.2	8.8	31.3	15.0	22.6	23.4
Semiskilled	13.5	5.2	28.8	3.4	24.9	14.6	18.6	2.6	23.1	8.4
Divisional Sector										
High-growth industries	48.2	100.0	37.2	100.0	25.2	100.0	41.0	100.0	54.2	100.0
Low-growth and stagnating	51.8	—	62.8	—	74.8	—	59.0	—	45.8	—

a. Data from the January 1986 Current Population Survey. All data refer to individuals aged 20–61 in January 1986. Displaced workers lost or left a full-time, private, nonagricultural, wage-salary job between January 1981 and January 1986 because of a plant closing, permanent reduction in force, or slack work, without recall as of January 1986.

likely to be employed in professional and other white-collar jobs than their displaced counterparts. Moreover, this general pattern tends to be much greater in some regions than others. In particular, displaced workers residing in the East North Central states appear to be much less well matched to growing industries than displaced workers in other regions. Just over a quarter had been previously employed in a growth sector at the time of layoff, compared to 54 percent of those from the West South Central states, and 48 percent of those from New England. Additionally, East North Central workers are overrepresented in blue-collar jobs and underrepresented in high-level, white-collar occupations when compared to both growth-sector workers in their region and displaced workers from other regions. It is not surprising, then, to find variations in the ability of these workers to obtain comparable-wage jobs (table 3.14).

Among the reemployed high-wage workers, those who had the highest probability of remaining in the high-wage quartile resided in the South Atlantic (69 percent) and New England (64 percent). Predictably, those least likely to maintain their position in the high-wage quartile resided in the West South Central (37 percent) and the East North Central (48 percent) regions. These patterns held up for skilled and semiskilled blue-collar workers, with the exception of the East North Central division. In the East North Central, 78 percent of the skilled workers and 57 percent of the semiskilled who were reemployed either maintained their position in the high-wage quartile or moved down into the high-middle quartile. These success rates were among the highest across the five divisions, lending support to the notion that workers in the East North Central division are reluctant or unable to change occupation and thus risk downward wage mobility.

But it still remains that workers in all regions change occupations and industries infrequently. Despite differences in economic conditions and the rate and nature of economic change, the regional results present strong evidence of the movement of displaced workers back to their old fields of work. In all cases, this appears linked to regional economic conditions and human capital mismatches between displaced and other workers within each of the quartiles of the wage and salary

Table 3.14
Postdisplacement Earnings Mobility for High-Wage Displaced Workers, by Selected Census Divisions[a]

	New England	Mid- Atlantic	East North Central	South Atlantic	West South Central
Highest Divisional Earnings Quartile on Former Job					
All Displaced Reemployed in:					
Lowest-quartile	7.1	15.5	9.1	8.7	7.0
Low-middle quartile	14.0	14.0	18.8	5.5	16.9
High-middle quartile	14.4	17.9	24.6	17.0	39.3
Highest-quartile	64.4	52.5	47.5	68.7	36.8
(% reemployed)	(85.6)	(70.8)	(80.4)	(76.7)	(83.4)
Skilled Blue-Collar Reemployed in:					
Lowest-quartile	6.6	13.0	4.5	5.2	12.4
Low-middle quartile	21.6	24.1	15.7	6.5	18.7
High-middle quartile	35.0	29.9	21.7	24.6	43.4
Highest-quartile	36.7	33.0	58.1	63.7	25.5
(% reemployed)	(100.0)	(67.5)	(77.7)	(70.3)	(85.0)
Semiskilled Blue-Collar Reemployed in:					
Lowest-quartile	0.0	33.2	21.9	23.6	18.7
Low-middle quartile	41.5	11.6	20.7	19.9	21.4
High-middle quartile	0.0	22.2	30.5	16.2	39.6
Highest-quartile	58.5	33.0	26.9	40.4	20.4
(% reemployed)	(91.5)	(52.8)	(81.6)	(72.8)	(71.7)
White-Collar and Service Reemployed in:					
Lowest-quartile	9.8	8.2	5.0	6.2	1.2
Low-middle quartile	0.0	10.3	20.4	0.5	14.8
High-middle quartile	5.9	10.0	23.5	12.9	37.7
Highest-quartile	84.3	71.6	51.1	80.3	46.3
(% reemployed)	(77.7)	(83.2)	(82.4)	(82.2)	(87.8)

a. Data from the January 1986 Current Population Survey. All data refer to individuals aged 20–61 in January 1986. Displaced workers lost or left a full-time, private, nonagricultural, wage-salary job between January 1981 and January 1986 because of a plant closing, permanent reduction in force, or slack work, without recall as of January 1986.

distribution. In some regions, these differences have become so large that workers have very little prospect of transferring their human capital to new, comparable-wage jobs. Especially for high-wage workers, the only choice left is to engage in a long-term search for reemployment opportunities in the layoff occupation and industry or risk a substantial earnings loss. While policies can be developed to help workers upgrade their education and skills for comparable-wage jobs, they would represent a sharp departure from the traditional, limited investment strategy used to date.

Pulling the Pieces Together: A Multivariate Analysis

To this point, we have seen several pieces of a complex puzzle describing the reemployment and earnings outcomes following displacement. It has been suggested that growing human capital gaps between declining and growing sectors have contributed to limited worker mobility and earnings losses. These gaps are evident throughout the wage and salary distribution of employment, particularly in higher-wage jobs, and in those regions of the country experiencing large declines in goods-producing industries and blue-collar employment.

A key result implied by these findings is that movement into growing as well as comparable-wage jobs declines with predisplacement earnings. Higher-wage workers laid off from blue-collar jobs do not appear to have the training and education needed to obtain new high-wage jobs. As a result, they tend not to pursue reemployment in growth sectors, and instead search for jobs in the industries and occupations from which they were laid off. In contrast, lower-wage workers are better matched to new job opportunities, but are also at an educational disadvantage.

Recent studies of worker displacement have confirmed the important role of education and training in the labor market.[10] In most cases, both factors have been shown to be positively related to postlayoff reemployment and earnings, and negatively associated with earning loss. From a policy perspective, this suggests that educational upgrading and occupational training are needed in any set of programs designed to facilitate successful readjustment following layoff.

Indeed, most policy analysts have concluded this and argued that training and education are needed to help laid-off workers find new jobs in the economy's growth sectors. And on a general level, our findings on occupational and educational upgrading also support this assertion. It is clear that in today's labor market, limited education and skills place one at a distinct disadvantage.

Despite this, it is also quite plausible that the limited movement of many displaced workers into growth sectors cannot be overcome with a single prescription of educational upgrading and skills training. As we discussed in chapter 2, growth industries are producing a variety of high- and lower-wage jobs that can accommodate workers with various education and training backgrounds. This would suggest that, holding other factors constant, education and training will not necessarily limit or facilitate entry into the economy's growth industries. Entry could be limited, however, if workers search for jobs that rely on their existing skills. Especially among higher-wage workers, there are large mismatches between the skills of the displaced and those required in growing industries.

If this is the case, then the policy implications become more complex. While it remains true that all workers can benefit from education and training, potentially costly investments may be required to help higher-wage workers adjust to changes in the structure of job opportunities. Absent training for new, comparable-wage jobs, the policy alternatives turn on helping workers return to the field from which they were laid off or obtain a lower-paying job in a growth industry. Lower-wage workers, in contrast, seem to be in a better position to benefit from a more modest investment strategy since they are better matched to jobs in growing sectors. Moreover, insofar as flexible labor market adjustment includes transitions from declining to growing sectors, the evidence would suggest that a mixed investment strategy may well be required.

In light of the strength of the findings presented thus far and their policy implications, we subjected them to more rigorous statistical testing. Specifically, we examined three key outcomes of interest that reflect the broad policy goals which seem to be achievable with varying degrees of difficulty. The first outcome (and that studied most often) is reemployment. "Reemployment" in this case is assessed in January 1986, for workers losing full-time jobs over the previous five years. The second outcome considered is reemployment in a divisional growth sector, which may improve economic efficiency and heighten future job security. Unlike reemployment alone, this outcome has received little attention in studies of worker displacement. The third outcome is reemployment in the same or higher divisional earnings quartile. This may be the most difficult outcome to achieve, but—at least in the short term—it is most desirable from the worker's point of view. Earnings comparability is assessed for full-time workers losing jobs which were in the highest three divisional earnings quartiles, who subsequently were reemployed as of January 1986.

These three outcomes are "binary choice variables"—a displaced worker is either reemployed or not; reemployed in a growth sector or not; or reemployed in a comparable-wage job or in a lower-wage job. Accordingly, a probit model was used to estimate the probabilities, while controlling for a standard set of worker characteristics and labor market conditions which may influence the three outcomes, including: age, education, race, industry, occupation, marital status, presence of children under 6, sex, and tenure on the former job. In addition, we also controlled for reason of displacement, receipt of advance notice of layoff, year of displacement, and state personal income growth over the 1979 to 1985 period.[11]

Of particular interest, given the earlier findings, is the influence of human capital characteristics, (including educational background, job tenure, and prior industry/occupation), and regional economic conditions (reflected by growth in state personal income). These results are presented in table 3.15 and discussed below.

Consistent with previous research, our findings show that the probability of reemployment increases with education, declines with age, and is relatively more difficult for blue-collar and manufacturing workers than white-collar service workers. Tenure is also inversely related to reemployment, reflecting the difficulty those with long-term stable attachments to a particular firm have in finding new jobs. Similar results are also evident with respect to the probability of reemployment in the same or a higher wage and salary quartile. The less educated, blue-collar, manufacturing workers with substantial tenure all have significantly more difficulty than their counterparts finding jobs that offer wages comparable to those received in the layoff job. As discussed earlier, these results point to the general need for educational upgrading and occupational training in programs designed to facilitate the transition of laid-off workers into new jobs.[12]

As expected, however, the results also reveal that neither education nor age have a statistically significant effect on the probability of reemployment in a growth sector. What does matter, and to a very large extent, is one's prior occupational and industry attachment. Rel-

Table 3.15
Estimated Probabilities of Reemployment Outcomes for Workers Displaced from Full-Time Jobs Between January 1981 and January 1986

	Reemployed in January 1986	Reemployed in a divisional growth sector, January 1986	Reemployed in the same or higher divisional wage quartile[a]
Baseline probabilities for workers with baseline characteristics:[b]	72.9%***	75.2%***	70.5%***
Impact on Probabilities of:			
Age			
20–24	+4.4**	+2.8	+3.2
45–61	−10.3***	−3.2*	−2.4
Reference group: 25–44			
Education			
<12 years education	−12.6***	−1.2	−13.7***
16–18 years education	+7.5***	+2.8	+13.3***
Reference Group: 12–14			
Type of Layoff Job			
Manufacturing	+2.0	−27.3***	−1.2
Reference group: non-manufacturing			
Skilled blue-collar	−3.2*	−14.1***	−4.4*
Semiskilled blue-collar	−6.4***	−11.8***	−5.6**
Reference group: white collar			
Years of Job Seniority			
4–9 years	4.7***	−4.0**	−4.8**
10–19 years	0.4	−4.4**	−10.6***
20+ years	−9.1***	−3.2	−18.4***
Reference group: <4			
Year Displaced			
1982	−0.4	−2.8	−7.1***
1983	−2.0	0.4	−6.4**
1984	−6.8***	−3.6*	−6.0*
1985	−27.0***	−6.0***	−5.2*
Reference group: 1981			
Real State Personal Income Growth, 1979–85			
Low-growth (10.4%)	−1.6***	+0.4	−2.0***
High-growth (22.4%)	+1.6***	−0.4	+2.0***
Changed Major Occupation	—	—	−16.6***

NOTE: See appendix 3A for full results of the Probit Estimations. Probabilities estimated from Z values of the normal distribution.

a. For those losing jobs in the three highest earnings quartiles, conditional upon reemployment in 1/86.

b. Baseline characteristics include: unmarried, nonwhite male, high school graduate, age 25–34, lost white-collar or service job in a service-producing sector in 1981 through a layoff without advance notice, less than 4 years seniority, real state personal income growth 1979–85 at U.S. average (16.4%).

*** Significant at 99 percent

**   Significant at 95 percent

*   Significant at 90 percent

ative to service and white-collar workers, those from the manufacturing sector with blue-collar skills are, holding other factors constant, substantially less likely to enter a growth sector. Moreover, the estimated probabilities for these groups are anywhere between 2 and 13 times larger than those obtained from the reemployment model. We can thus see that while growth industries have jobs for individuals with limited as well as advanced education and experience, they are less attractive or accessible to those from the industrial sector.

These findings help to explain why many blue-collar and manufacturing workers experience relatively long durations of joblessness. They also lend support to our earlier results suggesting that, at least in the eyes of the worker, comparable-wage reemployment is the most preferred reemployment outcome. The existence of skill mismatches at comparable-wage levels makes entry into growing industries a formidable challenge that only increases with one's earnings on the layoff job.

Earlier, we presented evidence suggesting that postlayoff adjustment varies according to economic conditions and improves over time. These results are largely substantiated in the probit models. First, the probability of reemployment does, indeed, increase with time. While workers laid off in 1982 or 1983 were just as likely to be reemployed in January 1986 as those laid off in 1981, the 1984 job-losers were 7 percent less likely than their 1981 counterparts to find a job. Those laid off in 1985 were 27 percent less likely to have found a job by January 1986.

While time also appears to have influenced the probability of reemployment in a growth sector, its effect is noticeably smaller than in the case of reemployment. In a similar fashion, economic conditions have no effect on the likelihood of reemployment. These results further support our earlier findings that the transition from declining to growing sectors can be quite difficult for many displaced workers. Even in growing states, displaced workers are not any more likely to become reemployed in a growth industry than they are in sluggish areas. And while time does increase the probability, it seems that it works in favor of reemployment in a nongrowth sector.

These findings have two important policy implications. The first is that the transition from declining to growing sectors, a key attribute of flexible labor market adjustment, is difficult for many workers. Those from the manufacturing sector are nearly 30 percent less likely to move into a growth-sector job than service sector employees, while blue-collar workers are between 12 and 14 percent less likely than their counterparts to do the same. While time and favorable economic conditions improve reemployment and earnings prospects, they are less important in influencing movement into a growth industry. To the extent that these intersector transitions are viewed as important goals of employment policy, it is clear that achieving them represents a formidable challenge.

The second implication is that the readjustment needs of workers varies as do the policy options available to address them. On the one hand, the evidence presented in this chapter suggests the less educated, older, and high-tenure worker will require special assistance in obtaining reemployment. For these workers, and for lower-wage workers as well, reemployment options can include relatively modest investments in education and training for a wide variety of jobs in growing and declining sectors. For example, holding other factors constant, helping the less educated attain a high school diploma can increase the probability of reemployment by nearly 13 percentage points.

On the other hand, the findings indicate that providing assistance to manufacturing and blue-collar workers can be more complex and potentially more costly. For one thing, programs will have to overcome the limited probability these workers have of entering growing industries. Since this appears linked to skills mismatches that rise with earnings, programs have two basic options: (1) intensive and costly retraining and educational upgrading for growth-sector jobs; or (2) reemployment in a field similar to that from which a worker was laid off. A third option is to assist a worker in lowering his or her expectations and provide assistance in preparing for and finding "a job."

Given this, it would appear that the current policy approach of limited program investments will not be sufficient for all workers. While those losing relatively low-wage manufacturing jobs do stand to benefit from modest boosts to their education and training, higher-wage, blue-collar workers are another matter. These workers face such substantial gaps in their human capital, that it is unlikely that existing policies and programs can help them overcome their competitive disadvantage and obtain comparable-wage jobs. It would seem that unless policymakers are willing to explicitly accept earnings losses and the social and personal costs that result from them as program outcomes, a different framework will have to be developed to support flexible labor market adjustment.

NOTES

1. "Semiskilled," blue-collar occupations include operatives, assemblers, transportation handlers, and laborers.

2. This translates into a national estimate of nearly 9 million displaced workers.

3. The layoff wages of displaced workers were inflated using the CPI to their January, 1986 equivalents.

4. See, for example, Francis W. Horvath, "The Pulse of Economic Change: Displaced Workers of 1981–85," *Monthly Labor Review* (June 1987); and Michael Podgursky and Paul Swaim, "Job Displacement and Earnings Loss: Evidence From the Displaced Worker Survey," *Industrial and Labor Relations Review* (October 1987).

5. See Christopher J. Ruhm, "The Economic Consequences of Labor Mobility," *Industrial and Labor Relations Review* (October 1987); and Janice F. Madden, "The Distribution of Economic Losses Among Displaced Workers: Measurement Methods Matter," *Journal of Human Resources* (Winter 1988).

6. While this is comparable to the experience of all displaced workers, the fact remains that high-wage, skilled, blue-collar workers experienced very long durations of joblessness. Over 37 percent reported being out of work for at least 27 weeks, in comparison to 29 percent of all workers and 17 percent of executive and professional workers.

7. To conduct this test, we relied on the same regression models presented in chapter 2. See appendix 2-B for the detailed results.

8. See appendix 3-A, table 3A-1 for regional reemployment rates by industry, occupation, and selected worker characteristics.

9. See table 3.9.

10. See: Michael Podgursky and Paul Swaim, "Job Displacement and Earnings Loss," *Industrial and Labor Relations Review*, 41, 1 (October 1987).

11. The full probit results are presented in appendix 3-A.

12. We further tested for the importance of human capital and other variables by re-estimating the reemployment probit models for workers laid off from each quartile of the wage and salary distribution. The findings support the general results reported here. See tables 3A-3 and 3A-4 for the detailed findings.

Appendix 3-A
Detailed Probit Results of
Reemployment Probabilities and
Other Supporting Tables

Table 3A-1
Reemployment and Total Weeks of Unemployment Since Lost Job, by Selected Census Divisions, 1986

	27+ total weeks of unemployment since last job					Reemployed full time, January 1986				
	New England	Mid-Atlantic	East North Central	South Atlantic	West South Central	New England	Mid-Atlantic	East North Central	South Atlantic	West South Central
All Full-Time Displaced	23.4	36.2	42.3	26.8	26.4	65.8	54.9	56.4	63.8	63.2
Industry										
Manufacturing	26.5	42.6	47.5	31.1	33.5	63.3	54.8	55.2	61.0	64.2
Other goods-producing	15.7	25.3	32.0	39.9	25.1	64.4	54.8	54.7	65.3	63.9
Trans., comm., util.	15.7	32.0	47.4	14.5	20.2	66.3	64.5	60.3	58.9	66.4
Trade	17.8	26.7	34.5	24.8	22.7	67.3	61.0	57.5	64.1	66.2
FIRE	41.6	23.4	43.0	12.4	7.8	68.4	59.2	56.3	82.0	70.8
Other services	18.6	30.0	32.6	19.6	12.6	74.6	45.9	60.1	69.5	51.0
Occupation										
Executive, prof., and mgr.	21.2	27.8	26.6	15.8	15.9	68.5	63.4	65.6	77.5	66.4
Technical	20.3	9.0	44.0	15.9	12.5	100.0	85.1	72.4	81.7	73.2
Sales	20.1	21.5	25.2	15.7	26.4	77.7	66.3	63.6	63.2	69.5
Admin. support/clerical	19.8	33.6	44.8	17.5	24.0	55.6	56.8	58.9	62.6	62.0
Craft and repair	15.0	35.0	44.3	27.2	29.8	74.2	60.0	55.2	67.1	67.4
Semiskilled	31.1	46.0	49.6	35.0	31.2	59.5	47.4	51.9	58.3	58.6
Education										
Less than high school graduate	24.5	43.9	55.6	44.0	34.3	50.2	32.4	41.6	49.7	53.2
High school graduate	24.3	39.6	41.1	23.5	25.2	65.4	58.5	52.4	64.0	60.8
1–3 years post-high school	19.0	28.0	40.6	14.4	27.9	73.2	57.6	66.3	76.1	68.4
4 + years post-high school	24.5	22.2	26.8	19.3	14.6	76.6	71.1	82.6	77.8	78.2
Sex										
Male	21.1	32.3	39.5	22.4	22.9	76.2	59.2	63.1	71.2	66.4
Female	27.2	42.9	48.7	35.0	33.5	48.8	47.3	40.5	50.6	56.6
Age										
20–24	7.6	21.6	24.8	20.0	14.7	68.5	55.3	49.0	50.5	62.8
25–34	19.8	34.7	40.1	24.8	26.6	60.8	59.0	59.8	68.2	64.5
35–44	23.3	40.0	48.8	27.6	31.2	82.7	59.8	60.4	67.8	69.4
45–54	34.3	36.1	46.2	25.4	26.5	58.1	47.5	56.3	65.2	57.6
55–61	38.9	50.9	56.9	51.4	36.9	58.3	41.4	40.9	45.0	40.2

Table 3A-2
Probit Maximum Likelihood Estimates of Reemployment Probabilities
for Workers Displaced From Full-Time Jobs, January 1981–January 1986

	Maximum likelihood estimates		
Coefficient	Reemployed in January 1986	Reemployed in a divisional growth sector, 1/86	Reemployed in the same or higher divisional earnings quartile[a]
Intercept	.493***	.694***	.412***
	(5.00)	(6.87)	(2.58)
Age 20–24	.116**	.075	.083
	(1.92)	(1.21)	(0.78)
Age 35–44	−.017	−.022	−.069
	(−0.35)	(−0.46)	(−1.01)
Age 45–61	−.261***	−.077*	−.065
	(−4.60)	(−1.32)	(0.76)
<12 years education	−.316***	−.025	−.351***
	(−6.47)	(−0.48)	(−4.08)
13–15 years education	.085**	.006	.031
	(1.69)	(0.11)	(0.44)
16–18 years education	.187***	.068	.338***
	(2.95)	(1.08)	(3.92)
White	.199***	−.021	.070
	(3.58)	(−0.37)	(0.71)
Female	−.250***	.141***	−.321***
	(−6.06)	(3.25)	(−4.71)
Married	.053	−.026	.174***
	(1.26)	(−0.61)	(2.66)
Children <6	−.197***	−.054	.073
	(−4.10)	(−1.09)	(1.02)
Lost job:			
Manufacturing	.045	−.747***	−.029
	(1.05)	(−17.17)	(−0.45)
Other goods-producing	−.117**	−.013	−.140*
	(−1.90)	(−0.20)	(−1.55)
Skilled blue-collar	−.076*	−.359***	−.113*
	(−1.35)	(−6.30)	(−1.38)
Semiskilled blue-collar	−.161***	−.298***	−.137**
	(−3.34)	(−6.08)	(−1.82)
4–9 years seniority	.116***	−.097**	−.117**
	(2.45)	(−2.06)	(−1.78)
10–19 years seniority	−.010	−.112**	−.273***
	(−0.16)	(−1.71)	(−3.02)
20+ years seniority	−.232***	−.075	−.485***
	(−2.35)	(−0.69)	(−3.08)
Plant closed	.101***	−.004	−.048
	(2.66)	(−0.10)	(−0.85)
Advance notice of job loss	.067**	−.011	.108**
	(1.82)	(−0.29)	(1.96)
Year displaced: 1982	−.010	−.067	−.182**
	(−0.15)	(−1.02)	(−2.05)
1983	−.046	.014	−.157**
	(−0.69)	(0.21)	(−1.70)

Table 3A-2 continued

Coefficient	Maximum likelihood estimates		
	Reemployed in January 1986	Reemployed in a divisional growth sector, 1/86	Reemployed in the same or higher divisional earnings quartile[a]
1984	−.167***	−.086*	−.150*
	(−2.56)	(−1.30)	(−1.64)
1985	−.745***	−.149***	−.129*
	(−12.33)	(−2.43)	(−1.38)
Real state personal income	.007***	−.001	.008***
	(3.73)	(−0.51)	(2.83)
Changed major occupation	—	—	−.431***
			(−7.67)
N	5,294	4,879	2,262
(−2.0) * log likelihood ratio	579.9	634.3	229.6

a. For those losing jobs in the three highest divisional earnings quartiles, conditional on reemployment in January 1986.

*** Null hypothesis of $H_0 = 0$ rejected at the 1% level.

** Null hypothesis of $H_0 = 0$ rejected at the 5% level.

* Null hypothesis of $H_0 = 0$ rejected at the 10% level.

Table 3A-3
**Estimated Reemployment Probabilities, by Former
Earnings Quartiles of Dislocated Workers**

	Divisional earnings quartile (former job)			
	Lowest	**Low-middle**	**High-middle**	**Highest**
Baseline probability of reemployment[a]	64.1%**	63.3%**	60.6%*	61.4%*
Impact on reemployment of:				
Age				
20–24	+8.3%**	+8.3%**	+6.4%*	+9.9%**
45–61	−12.2%***	−12.2%***	−13.7%***	−12.2%**
Education				
<12 years education	−10.3%***	−11.0%***	−11.4%***	−12.9%***
16–18 years education	+13.7%***	+12.9%***	+7.9%*	+9.1%*
Type of Layoff Job				
Manufacturing	+0.4%	+0.8%	−0.8%	−1.2%
Skilled blue-collar	+2.0%	+2.0%	+0.4%	+0.8%
Semiskilled blue-collar	−2.0%	−2.0%	−3.6%	−4.0%
Years of Job Seniority				
4–9 years	+0.4%	+0.4%	+0.8%	+0.8%
10–19 years	−4.8%	−6.8%	−1.2%	+1.6%
20+ years	+14.8%*	+15.9%*	+16.3%*	+14.1%
Year Displaced				
1982	+2.8%	+1.2%	+3.2%	−0.4%
1983	−1.2%	−2.8%	+2.0%	+2.4%
1984	+0.4%	−1.6%	+0.8%	−3.6%
1985	−27.0%***	−28.2%***	−27.9%***	−31.1%***
Real State Personal Income Growth, 1979–85				
Low-growth (10.4%)	−0.8%**	−0.8**	−0.8%**	−0.8%*
High-growth (22.4%)	+0.8%**	+0.8**	+0.8%**	+0.8%*

a. See table 3.15 for complete description of baseline characteristics. Baseline age is 25–34 years; baseline education is 12 years; baseline occupation is white-collar or service; baseline state personal income growth is the national average (16.4%). Full Probit results reported in table 3A-4.

*** Significant at 99 percent

** Significant at 95 percent

* Significant at 90 percent

Table 3A-4
Probit Maximum Likelihood Estimates of Reemployment,
by Earnings Quartile on Former Job
(*t*-statistics in parenthesis)

	Maximum likelihood estimates			
	Former earnings quartile			
	Lowest	Low-middle	High-middle	Highest
Intercept	.357**	.340**	.273*	.294*
	(1.86)	(1.71)	(1.30)	(1.32)
Age 20–24	.211**	.209**	.158*	.252**
	(2.08)	(1.98)	(1.40)	(2.02)
Age 35–44	−.037	.000	−.069	−.063
	(−0.36)	(0.00)	(−0.61)	(−0.52)
Age 45–61	−.308***	−.314***	−.345***	−.309**
	(−2.64)	(−2.61)	(−2.64)	(−2.25)
<12 years education	−.260***	−.284***	−.294***	−.332***
	(−2.81)	(−2.98)	(−2.91)	(−3.03)
13–15 years education	.231**	.208**	.169*	.183*
	(2.25)	(1.94)	(1.45)	(1.45)
16–18 years education	.346***	.334***	.201*	.227*
	(2.53)	(2.41)	(1.34)	(1.45)
White	.026	.041	.127	.108
	(0.25)	(0.38)	(1.11)	(0.86)
Female	−.170**	−.188**	−.083	−.026
	(−1.90)	(−2.03)	(−0.78)	(−0.23)
Married	.219***	.251***	.329***	.349***
	(2.63)	(2.87)	(3.43)	(3.40)
Children <6	−.270***	−.188**	−.194**	−.132
	(−2.73)	(−2.04)	(−1.72)	(−1.09)
Lost job:				
Manufacturing	.011	.018	−.021	−.032
	(0.14)	(0.21)	(−0.23)	(−0.33)
Other goods-producing	.018	.021	−.017	−.003
	(0.14)	(0.16)	(−0.12)	(−0.02)
Skilled blue-collar	.052	.055	.008	.021
	(0.42)	(0.44)	(0.07)	(0.16)
Semiskilled blue-collar	−.053	−.048	−.092	−.105
	(−0.54)	(−0.48)	(−0.90)	(−0.96)
4–9 years seniority	.012	.008	.020	.019
	(0.11)	(0.08)	(0.18)	(0.16)
10–19 years seniority	−.121	−.170	−.034	.036
	(−0.79)	(−1.07)	(−0.20)	(0.20)
20+ years seniority	.381*	.412*	.417*	.357
	(1.45)	(1.51)	(1.47)	(1.22)
Plant closed	.183***	.189***	.211***	.252***
	(2.44)	(2.43)	(2.54)	(2.83)
Advance notice of job loss	.017	.019	.018	.049
	(0.23)	(0.26)	(0.22)	(0.57)
Year displaced: 1982	.068	.034	.079	−.008
	(0.51)	(0.24)	(0.53)	(−0.05)
1983	−.031	−.072	.054	.056
	(−0.23)	(−0.50)	(0.35)	(0.33)
1984	.011	−.038	.015	−.093

Table 3A-4 continued

| | Maximum likelihood estimates | | | |
| | Former earnings quartile | | | |
	Lowest	Low-middle	High-middle	Highest
	(0.08)	(−0.28)	(0.10)	(−0.59)
1985	−.742***	−.781***	−.771***	−.875***
	(−6.12)	(−6.20)	(−5.84)	(−6.06)
Real state personal income	.008**	.008**	.008**	.007*
growth, 1979–85	(2.03)	(2.10)	(1.75)	(1.50)
Reemployment rate	.558	.634	.674	.664
N	1,377	1,291	1,143	1,015
(−2.0) * log likelihood	246.5	161.6	111.7	137.3

*** Null hypothesis of $H_0 = 0$ rejected at the 1% level.

** Null hypothesis of $H_0 = 0$ rejected at the 5% level.

* Null hypothesis of $H_0 = 0$ rejected at the 10% level.

4
Creating a Responsive Policy Strategy

By this point, three developments in the U.S. labor market should be clear. The first is that, since 1979, unprecedented changes in the structure of job opportunities have occurred. This has been illustrated by the shift from blue- to white-collar employment, a decline in the growth of jobs in the middle of the wage and salary distribution, and substantial educational and skill upgrading in all jobs, and especially in higher-wage jobs. In some regions of the country, such as the Midwest, these changes have been much more pronounced and visible than in others. But in all areas, significant changes in the types and mix of jobs have occurred. This is not a new trend per se, but it is one that accelerated since the early 1980s.

The second development is that the labor market is not as flexible as what might be desired. Although the free flow of workers from declining to growing sectors is desirable from an efficiency perspective, the evidence indicates that intersector mobility occurs infrequently. Overall, large proportions of displaced workers wind up finding new jobs in the same general sector from which they were laid off. Workers losing jobs in slow-growing sectors tend to remain in those sectors, and blue-collar workers, for the most part, return to blue-collar employment. While it is true that these and other workers do change industries and occupations, most of the changes are in the same broad sectors in which the layoff occurred. Worker mobility in the U.S. cannot be characterized by high levels of movement between declining and growing sectors of the economy.

The third development is that worker adjustment to economic change has been difficult and costly. Following layoff, some 30 percent of displaced workers are without work for more than 27 weeks, and one-third experience an earnings decline sufficient in size to drop them down at least one quartile in the wage and salary distribution. Moreover, earnings losses remain substantial even after controlling for differences in human capital and personal characteristics between displaced and other workers. Our estimates indicate that the reemployment earnings of displaced workers are 15 to 20 percent below those of other workers, and that these losses persist over time. While the findings do suggest that earnings recovery increases with time, it still takes the average male displaced worker five years to recoup fully his earnings, and at least two years to recover 50 percent of the loss.

These results suggest that federal policies are needed to speed up the reemployment process and help displaced workers limit their earnings loss. Long-term unemployment and earnings losses that are sustained for several years imply market imperfections that cannot be overcome easily by individual workers themselves. While it is true that many workers eventually recoup their earnings, this does not diminish the need for government assistance. Despite improving economic conditions and recall, it remains the case that several years transpire before workers are able to fully recover from a layoff.

It is possible that workers experience earnings loss because they were overpaid on the layoff job relative to others with similar characteristics. This could result from union affiliation, interindustry wage differentials, or selective layoff due to poor performance or low productivity.[1] Under any of these scenarios, the reemployment focus of federal policies would remain clear, but the case for limiting earnings loss would be weakened. For the policymaker, the question would become whether society should bear the full cost of helping workers make up lost economic rents.

There is no doubt that economic rents are lost by many displaced workers. But as we discussed in chapter 2, it is also true that the size of these rents can be expected to vary substantially, and that not all are positive. Moreover, the issue of rents tends to be most associated with certain worker subgroups, and not all displaced workers. Overall, available evidence suggests that earnings decline cannot be attributed wholly to the loss of rents enjoyed on the layoff job.[2] There does seem to be a strong reason for concern over the declining earnings of displaced workers. And it appears that changes in the structure and location of job opportunities are playing an important role in shaping this problem.

Throughout the last two chapters, we have compiled evidence strongly suggesting that shifts in the structure and geographic location of jobs have presented displaced workers with substantial postlayoff adjustment difficulties. Within and across the wage and salary distribution of employment as well as industry sectors, we have seen educational and occupational upgrading occurring at a pace far more rapid than in previous periods. We have also seen sharp differences in the composition of growing and declining jobs and between displaced workers and their growth-sector counterparts. These trends are especially evident in the upper half of the wage and salary distribution of employment and in certain regions of the country, such as the midwestern states. Overall, employers in the economy's growing sectors are simply not looking for adult male workers with a limited education and industrial skills. To the contrary, they place a disproportionate emphasis on advanced education and training, a youthful and female workforce, and providing services rather than producing goods.

For the displaced worker, this creates the potential for a skills mismatch that cannot be overcome easily. On average, growth industries have proportionately few jobs that rely on the skills and education of the displaced worker. While there are some jobs that are a good fit, they represent a relatively small share of all growing jobs. Faced with this, a return to a slow-growing or declining sector may represent the best way for many displaced workers to obtain jobs that require their skills and experience.

Indeed, our results showed that, regardless of occupational background or region of residence, workers do become reemployed in the same general sectors from which they were laid off. As would be expected, workers who make a change are among those experiencing the greatest earnings declines. Unless workers are willing to wait for familiar jobs to develop, they will be faced with having to choose between making an investment in retraining, education, and perhaps relocation, or accepting a job that makes limited use of their skills and experience. In many cases, this means a drop down the earnings ladder.

This dilemma is at the heart of much of the difficulty faced by displaced workers. It helps to explain why earnings loss may occur and also points to the overall difficulty workers face in obtaining comparable-wage jobs. Such jobs indeed exist, but in many cases, they are so different from those formerly held by the displaced that substantial investments in retraining and education would be required to increase accessibility to them. While such investments may be desirable, their implied magnitude serves to question their feasibility for both the individual worker and federal policy.

As would be expected, large investments are not necessarily required for all displaced workers. Our results also indicate that worker adjustment to economic change varies by subgroup. In particular, there are certain groups which, following layoff, face considerable difficulty in simply finding another job. Less educated, older workers, those with accumulated tenure, and workers with blue-collar skills all have reemployment rates that are significantly lower than those of their counterparts. These same groups do not, however, necessarily experience equal difficulty in obtaining a comparable-wage job.

The ability of displaced workers to obtain comparable-wage jobs depends, in large part, on where they stood in the wage and salary distribution at the time of layoff. As we discussed in chapters 2 and 3, the problem of comparable-wage reemployment is most acute among those losing higher-wage jobs. Typically, the average high-wage worker in the U.S. is relatively well educated, has advanced training, and works in the service sector. In comparison, workers displaced from high-wage jobs earned that position largely through on-the-job skills that are not tied to formal educational achievement. Only one-quarter have a college diploma, nearly half have not gone beyond high school, and over 50 percent held blue-collar positions.

At lower wage levels, there are fewer disparities between the education and training backgrounds of displaced workers and those of either all full-time workers or growth-sector employees. Although such gaps exist, they have been shown to be smaller in magnitude. For the most part, displaced workers in the lower half of the wage and salary distribution are much better matched to new growing jobs than their higher-wage counterparts.

As a result, it is not surprising that earnings recovery varies inversely with layoff wages or that higher-wage workers have less intersector mobility than their lower-wage counterparts. The evidence indicates clearly that many higher-wage job-losers qualify for few of the white-collar service jobs available at comparable wages, while lower-wage workers have a broader spectrum of opportunities from which to choose. This problem of skills match is particularly acute for the less educated as well as those semiskilled blue-collar workers losing higher-wage jobs. While 49 percent of all high-wage workers found new, high-wage jobs, only 29 percent of semiskilled workers were able to do the same.

We can thus see that for many groups, relatively modest investments in remedial education, entry-level job training, and job search assistance can be potentially valuable. In particular, workers from the lower half of the wage and salary distribution appear most likely to be able to benefit from such an approach. While limited investments can also potentially help higher-wage displaced workers find another job, they will likely do little to offset this group's loss in earnings. For these workers, substantial investments in education and retraining will be required to increase accessibility to comparable-wage jobs. Although the size of such investments may well be outside the bounds that taxpayers have thus far been willing to authorize, this does not imply that comparable-wage reemployment is infeasible. It may simply mean that changes in existing programs are necessary or that new institutions and financing mechanisms for promoting flexible labor market adjustment are required.

If these developments were simply the result of the last recession, they could be viewed as temporary and requiring short-term labor market adjustment strategies. By all accounts, however, they are part of a longer-term trend which accelerated in the early 1980s, and which is projected to continue well into the future. Over the next several years, jobs are expected to change more frequently and demand more skills and training; at the same time, fewer workers will be available to fill them. Between now and the year 2000, the nation's labor force is projected to grow more slowly and age more quickly than at any time since the 1930s.[3] These trends will only heighten the importance of flexible labor market adjustment, particularly among experienced workers such as those recently displaced from their jobs.

This creates a policy context that cannot be viewed as short term or necessarily focused solely on displaced workers. While recent job-losers are indeed in need of assistance, their problems can also be seen as a reflection of the types of challenges that the U.S. will have to face in the future. Educational upgrading, occupational retraining, and frequent job changing will become more the norm than an exception to an otherwise stable and uninterrupted career.

Within this context, the policy challenges are substantial. In the short term, displaced workers require assistance in finding new jobs, preferably ones that make use of their experience and skills. Over the longer term, however, these policies will have to evolve into a broader framework that can facilitate labor market adjustment on as well as off the job.

In this final chapter, we address these policy concerns by drawing on the findings presented in earlier chapters to sketch out a strategic response to continued economic change. We begin with the short-term policy issues and then move on to a larger policy framework for facilitating future flexible labor market adjustment.

Repositioning Existing Policy

Recently, the Congress enacted new trade legislation to strengthen the competitiveness of the American economy. Among the provisions of this legislation is a new program for displaced workers that replaces Title III of JTPA. The new program—the Economic Dislocation and Worker Adjustment Assistance Act (EDWAA)—is expected to bolster the economy's performance by facilitating the return of displaced workers to productive employment.

The EDWAA program is also designed to build upon the lessons learned under Title III. It contains a number of legislative provisions intended to strengthen the country's response to the labor market consequences of displacement. For one thing, the legislation recognizes the importance of income support to participation in training. While

Title III contained no provision for needs-based payments, EDWAA authorizes income support payments up to 25 percent of all program expenditures.

The new legislation is also intended to develop a closer link between worker adjustment programs and the unemployment insurance system. It requires coordination between the two programs and directly links the receipt of income support payments to a UI beneficiary's willingness to participate in training.

In addition to coordination, the new legislation contains a number of other provisions aimed at improving the delivery of programs. It requires the establishment of special rapid-response units in each state to address permanent business closures or mass layoffs, authorizes the use of flexible voucher certificates to purchase training for up to two years, and mandates that no less than 40 percent of the funds received by a state be allocated, by formula, to local areas.[4] Authorized at nearly one billion dollars, the EDWAA legislation is viewed as a major step in creating a national program to address worker displacement and facilitate flexible labor market adjustment.

What the legislation does not change, however, is the broad flexibility states and localities have in choosing who to serve and determining the services to offer. As with Title III, these decisions, as well as choices over program goals and objectives, remain a matter of state and local discretion. In some areas of the country, programs will emphasize retraining workers from specific industries or occupations, while in others, the emphasis may be on serving a steady flow of unemployment insurance recipients. But if history is any guide, the types of help workers receive under EDWAA will likely be similar to those provided under Title III. Programs will offer a mix of short-term, placement-oriented services together with educational remediation and skills training. On average, the investments will be modest and within conventional norms.[5]

As we have seen from the experience of displaced workers, this strategy will not necessarily fulfill the needs of all individuals or sectors of the economy. While it can readily fill vacancies by facilitating worker reemployment, it cannot as easily limit mismatches or earnings loss. Some workers, including the less educated and blue-collar workers losing higher-wage jobs, are simply not in a position to transfer their skills to new, comparable-wage jobs. The program expenditures and personal investments required to build new skills, and often new careers, may simply be too great to support within the framework of existing federal programs. These workers may still be able to derive benefits from relatively modest investments in training and education, however. Although they may experience large earnings losses, programs have the potential of helping these individuals to work and earn more than they would be able to on their own.

There are also other experienced workers who may be able to benefit from a short-term, modest investment strategy. As we discussed earlier, workers in the lower half of the wage distribution with limited education and from semiskilled and unskilled jobs may be in a position to benefit most from placement and training assistance in a wide variety of occupational fields. Because of the large number of growing jobs for which these workers qualify, programs can potentially help them find a new job and avoid large earnings losses.

To date, studies of the effectiveness of displaced worker programs have not focused on differences in impacts between high- and lower-wage workers. The findings from three recent large-scale evaluations indicate, however, that training and placement programs for displaced workers can increase employment and earnings. Overall, the three studies show positive and significant effects of program participation on postlayoff employment and earnings.[6] Although the magnitudes of the reported effects vary in size, they provide a strong reason to believe that training and placement programs of the type offered under JTPA can have a positive influence on the postlayoff adjustment process of displaced workers.[7] In one study, set in Buffalo, New York, the weekly earnings of program participants were estimated to have increased by $115, while another study of programs in Houston and El Paso, Texas, reported average quarterly earnings gains of $550.

At the same time, both the Texas and Buffalo studies report that program participants experienced large earnings losses relative to the layoff job.[8] Although these losses are not as great as they would have been in the absence of the program, they still represent significant declines. In the Buffalo evaluation, for example, 72 percent of program participants became reemployed in jobs offering weekly wages that paid no more than 75 percent of those received on the layoff jobs. In Texas, similar results emerged—one year after program participation, displaced workers were earning no more than roughly 60 percent of what they earned on the layoff job.

While neither study specifically analyzed earnings loss, it is instructive that each of the programs enrolled individuals who, by and large, were formerly employed in relatively high-wage jobs. In comparison to the $8.51 an hour earned by all production and nonsupervisory manufacturing workers in the U.S. during 1983, workers in the Buffalo program lost jobs paying an average of $10.78 per hour. In the Texas programs, 55 percent of enrolled workers earned $13.52 an hour on the layoff job. In view of the adjustment problems faced by higher-wage workers, the observed earnings losses are not surprising. As expected, they suggest that modest investments in training and placement programs can favorably impact earnings, but not to the degree needed to substantially restore lost earnings.[9]

Whether greater investments would yield more favorable results is unclear. The evidence available suggests that, at least within the range of investments made by JTPA, this may not be the case.[10] In each of the three evaluations, some effort was made to assess the relative effectiveness of job search assistance and the more costly classroom skills training. Although selection bias and other methodological considerations affected the findings of each study, they each reported little, if any difference in the effectiveness of the two program alternatives. Given that job search assistance is the less expensive of the two, it was reported consistently as the more cost-effective strategy.

Understanding why skills training does not appear to be as cost-effective as the less expensive job search assistance is a key issue warranting further investigation. All available evidence indicates that some amount of educational upgrading and retraining is critical for most dislocated workers. While the observed findings may reflect inefficiencies in program operations, they may also suggest the need for more costly and intensive training. In other words, for training to make a difference, especially for higher-wage workers, it may have to be substantially more intensive than what is currently offered by public employment and training programs.

The feasibility of extensive educational upgrading and occupational retraining is, however, unclear. On the one hand, public employment and training programs have had limited experience providing experienced, adult workers with costly, long-term education and training services. Moreover, participation in such programs can be costly for the worker who ultimately needs a job, and needs one relatively quickly. Although income support payments, such as unemployment insurance, are available to defray part of these costs, they are relatively short term and not sufficiently long to correspond with a program effort that may well require one or more years. Unless programs are able to shift their primary focus from daytime participation for unemployed workers to also include evening programs for many individuals who must return to work quickly, it may simply be impractical to consider increasing the cost and intensity of training programs.

On the other hand, even if it were feasible to offer long-term training and education services, the cost may simply be too great for society itself to incur. It may also not be fully warranted since many displaced workers are able to recoup their earnings over time. From an investment perspective, the benefits of additional training and education services would have to be balanced by the eventual self-recovery of many workers as well as the value of any lost economic rents.

If only implicitly, society has already addressed this issue. The public employment and training system for displaced workers acts much like a safety net; it catches workers affected by economic change and helps them get back on their feet and back to work. The costs of change—both economic and personal—are shared by the worker and society. In the current policy framework, society bears some of the cost of readjustment, but thus far, has not authorized spending levels sufficient to account for the full cost of economic change and individual adjustment to it.

In view of this, one option is to shift the policy focus from the individual to the family. In many respects, the family is the appropriate policy focus since displacement affects the labor force participation of its members as well as its overall income level and status.

Recent studies have revealed that displacement of married men stimulates employment and earnings among wives. In one recent study, for example, it was shown that increased labor force participation among wives helped to cushion part of a husband's lost earnings.[11] While this amounted to only 30 percent of the lost earnings in a quarter of all families, it provides some promise for policies aimed at increasing the employment and earnings of nonworking wives. Two-earner families are a common occurrence today, and have provided a vehicle for American families to maintain their standard of living.[12] To the extent that programs reorient their attention to the family unit, they can help displaced-worker families offset the earnings loss experienced by a spouse and maintain their standard of living as well.

Another option is to reconsider the current policy framework, including its financing. Publicly-financed training programs, such as Title III and the new EDWAA program, find it difficult to respond to changing education and skill requirements because they operate out of the flow of economic change and only after workers have been affected. Retraining and education policies outside the context of work cannot be expected to help workers fully prepare for new skill requirements, new jobs, or career changes. They can only "catch" workers at a time when the need for change is most pressing. At this point, practical considerations, public expectations, and cost constraints limit potential training and family investments and dictate relatively expedient solutions. As much value as this approach has, it falls short of representing a framework for facilitating adjustment to change. Policy needs to be repositioned from its exclusive focus on the effects of change to the process of change itself.

Forging Future Policy

All signals indicate that a new framework is needed to facilitate on- as well as off-the-job labor market adjustment. Continued economic restructuring, additional worker layoffs, a slow-growing and aging labor force, and increasing demands for a competent and flexible workforce will make ongoing training and development vital to both the economy and its workers. Yet in the U.S. today, virtually no public policy exists to stimulate training and education directly and on a continuing basis.

This is not because there is fundamental disagreement among policymakers over the importance of such goals. Nor is it the result of limited training institutions or ideas and proposals for how to best promote flexible labor force adjustment. It is now widely recognized that the future well-being of the economy and its workers will require policies that support adjustment to continued changes in the structure and content of jobs. And indeed, several proposals and ideas that would use the tax system to leverage on-the-job training and education funds have been developed.[13] Then why has policy development been so slow in moving? At the center of the problem are a complex set of issues that deal as much with basic policy principles and goals as they do with operations and administrative concerns.

For one thing, the issue of general versus specific training has served to muddy the policy waters by raising the question of who shall benefit from such policies. As things now stand, private employers have an interest in their workers acquiring skills and capabilities related directly to their jobs—this enhances on-the-job productivity and limits the extent to which workers can take their new skills to other competing employers. While workers can also benefit from specific training, the acquisition of more general skills and abilities is what is often needed to prepare for job and career changes, whether they be with an existing or new employer. Since tax dollars are typically viewed as the principal source of revenue to support more general on-the-job training and education, resolving this issue stands squarely in the path of new policy development. Moreover, the public demands, and rightly so, that financial support be withheld from activities that would have occurred in the absence of any intervention. Since it is well known that firms already support significant levels of on-the-job training, it is not clear whether new public monies will substitute for or expand that which already occurs.

These questions of policy purpose and control are exacerbated by the current division of responsibility for tax-based economic policies and those relying on existing public revenues and institutions. Currently in the Congress, there is one policy structure that deals with overall

economic and tax policy (e.g. Ways and Means, Economic Commit-
tees, the Treasury), and another that addresses human resources development policy through existing public bureaucracies (the Labor and
Human Resource Committee in the Senate and the Education and
Labor Committee in the House). Title III and the EDWAA program,
for example, fall into the latter group while tax policy to leverage
on-the-job education and training funds are the purview of the former
group. The problem is that these two policy groups have tended to
focus on complementary but different sets of issues. Because the
emerging need for on-the-job funding of skill and educational development borders the mission of both camps, policy development can
only be achieved if these two groups join forces on common ground.

Any effort to extend the public employment and training system
must contend with these issues. However, in doing so, one need not
presume that it is government's full responsibility to finance the costs
of such efforts. Is it not the case that individuals and employers also
benefit from continued education and training, and therefore have
some responsibility for cost sharing? If so, it would follow that one
role of public policy could be to stimulate such joint arrangements and
create a framework for continued training and education.

Some firms and organizations, most notably in the unionized sector,
have taken up these issues and provide at least one basic model for
others to consider. In the auto, steel, and telecommunications industries, for example, labor and management have used the collective
bargaining process to develop joint programs that support the continued development of employees.[14] While the nature of these programs
varies, the programs share several important characteristics. First, they
are all privately funded, in some cases by the companies and in others
by employees as well. Public funds, if they are used, represent only a
small share of total funding, and have been leveraged on the basis of
existing private resources and capabilities.

Second, these programs focus on both displaced workers and active
employees. In so doing, they recognize the readjustment problems of
laid-off employees as well as the importance of continued, on-the-job
training and development. Third, these initiatives stress individual
personal development as much as they do job-specific training. Last,

and perhaps most important, is that these joint programs represent an effort to recast the long held promise of job security in terms of career security. By providing workers with resources, information, and training, it is expected that they will be more prepared to cope with the changing needs of the workplace and adjust successfully to the forces of economic change and displacement.

Projecting such joint programs to other sectors, and particularly the nonunionized sector, is quite ambitious. Differences in political, cost, and competitive pressures suggest that replication will be difficult. But, it is clear that the constraints of public spending limit the types and nature of education and training that can be provided to workers on, as well as off, the job. Today's workers affected by economic change appear to require a level of assistance beyond that provided by public programs alone. And tomorrow's workers will also need assistance to support their continued adaptation to changes in the structure and content of jobs. Policymakers must therefore overcome institutional barriers to creative program strategies and devise new ways to stimulate the emergence of new structures to facilitate the process of economic change. Only then can the U.S. address successfully the dual challenge of facilitating productive adjustment and insulating workers from the negative consequences of economic change.

NOTES

1. Each of these explanations can also be used to explain the longer-term unemployment experienced by displaced workers. Faced with losing all or a portion of the economic rents they enjoyed on the layoff job, workers, and especially those from high-rent industries such as manufacturing, can be viewed as preferring to wait for another high-wage job to develop rather than take one offering lower wages. See, for example: Lawrence Summers, "Why is Unemployment So Very High Near Full Employment," *Brookings Papers on Economic Activity* 2, (1986).

2. See chapter 2 for a discussion of these points.

3. For a comprehensive review of projected labor force changes, see: William B. Johnston, *Workforce 2000: Work and Workers for the 21st Century*. Indianapolis: The Hudson Institute, 1987, chapter 3.

4. Under Title III, states had full discretion over how and to whom funds were allocated.

5. By this, we refer to the current average cost of serving participants in Title III programs.

6. See: Howard Bloom, et al., *Evaluation of the Worker Adjustment Demonstration: Final*

Report, Abt Associates Inc., Cambridge, MA, July 1986.

Walter Corson, et al., *An Impact Evaluation of the Buffalo Dislocated Worker Demonstration Program*, Mathematica Policy Research, Inc., Princeton, NJ, March 1985.

Jane Kulik, et al., *The Downriver Community Conference Economic Readjustment Program: Final Evaluation Report*, Abt Associates Inc., Cambridge, MA, May 1984.

7. For a critical review of these studies and a discussion of key findings, see: William Bowman, *Do Dislocated Worker Programs Work?*, Annapolis Research Center, Annapolis, MD, July 1986.

8. The Downriver study did not report on layoff and reemployment wages rates or earnings.

9. While the Buffalo and Texas studies did report on layoff and reemployment earnings, they did not disaggregate the data by layoff wages. It is thus not possible to examine separately earnings losses of program participants by their layoff earnings status.

10. In a recent study of 563 Title III projects funded under JTPA, the General Accounting Office found that the median duration of participation in classroom skills training was nine weeks with 32 percent of the projects offering services that lasted for less than six weeks. Median weeks of participation for remedial education was two weeks, while job search assistance programs did not operate with a fixed time frame. Nonetheless, participation in job search assistance was very short, with roughly one to two weeks of instruction and an open-ended invitation to seek employment. See: U.S. General Accounting Office, *Dislocated Workers: Local Programs and Outcomes Under the Job Training Partnership Act*, Washington, D.C., March 1987.

11. See: Adam Seitchik, *When Married Men Lose Jobs: Earnings Loss and Income Replacement in the New Family Economy*, Unpublished Working Paper, Wellesley College, Wellesley, MA, December, 1987.

12. See, for example: Frank Levy, "The Middle-Class: Is It Really Vanishing?" *Brookings Review* (January 1987).

13. See, for example: Harold Hovey, *The Role of Federal Tax Policy in Employment Policy*, National Governors' Association, Washington, D.C., January, 1985.

U.S. Departments of Labor and Treasury, *The Use of Tax Subsidies for Employment*, U.S. Government Printing Office, Washington, D.C., May, 1986.

Wayne Vroman, *Innovative Developments in Unemployment Insurance*, National Commission for Employment Policy, Washington, D.C., February, 1985.

14. For a review of recent joint labor-management human resources development programs, see: *From Vision to Reality*, UAW/Ford National Education Development and Training Center, Dearborn, MI, Spring 1985.

INDEX

Adjustment programs. *See* Economic Dislocation and Worker Adjustment Assistance Act (EDWAA); Job Training Partnership Act (JTPA); Transition programs, federal; Transition programs, private; workers, displaced

Bloom, Howard S., 12n.8, 12n.9, 124-25n.6
Blue-collar employment: decline in occupations for, 24; protection against layoff for, 30; shift to white-collar of, 111; *See also* Workers, displaced
Bowman, William, 125n.7
Bruno, Lee, 11n.5

Corson, Walter, 12n.8, 124-25n.6
Current Population Survey (CPS): Displaced Worker Supplement of, 10-11, 65-66; earnings information of, 31; March Work Experience Supplements to, 10, 20

Displaced workers. *See* Workers, displaced
Displacement effect on earnings, 31-34

Earnings: effect of loss of, 29-34; loss for displaced workers, 7-8; pattern for full-time workers, 27; *See also* Wage opportunities
Economic change: effect at regional level of, 46, 111; effect of, 1-3; worker adjustment to, 111-12, 114
Economic Dislocation and Worker Adjustment Assistance Act (EDWAA): as replacement for Title III of JTPA, 4, 8-9; provisions and limitations of, 116-18
Education: gap between declining and growth industries for, 3, 62; as improvement in human capital, 20-21, 23; investment in remedial, 115-16, 119-20; of long-term unemployed, 25-27; relationship to wage of 15-17
EDWAA. *See* Economic Dislocation and Worker Adjustment Assistance Act (EDWAA)
Employment: contribution of semiskilled jobs to growth of, 24; growth from 1970 to present, 13-14; pattern of growth and

decline in, 18-19; shift from manufacturing of, 3; shift from semiskilled, 21; *See also* Industry; Unemployment; Workers, displaced
Employment and Training Assistance for Dislocated Workers, 4
Employment assistance programs. *See* Public policy; Training programs; Transition programs, federal; Transition programs, private; Workers, displaced
Employment mobility: intersector infrequency of, 111; limitations for displaced workers of, 3, 9, 27
Employment opportunities: analysis of changing distribution of, 34-46; effect of shifts in structure of, 7, 15-18; human capital distribution of, 27; regional patterns of change for, 42

Freeman, Richard, 47n.8

Growth industries. *See* Industry

Hiring requirements. *See* Employment; Occupations; Workers, displaced
Horath, Francis W., 11n.2, 12n.10, 101n.4
Hovey, Harold, 125n.13
Human capital: differences affecting displaced workers, 7-8, 21, 23; improvement in U.S. stock of, 20; transferability for displaced workers of, 78

Industry: change for displaced workers of, 68; divergence between growth and nongrowth, 25, 35-39; educational requirements for growth, 62; sectors of growth in, 51-54; workers in growth, 26
Industry transition: means to achieve, 61-62
Investment: in human capital for comparable-wage reemployment, 78

Jacobson, Louis, 47n.10
Jobs. *See* Occupations
Job search assistance: under EDWAA, 9; value of, 115

127

Job training: entry-level, 115; for new occupations, 116, 119-20

Job Training Partnership Act (JTPA): eligibility for, 4; goal, intent, costs and expenditures for, 5-6, 20; placement rates under, 7; services of, 20

Johnston, William B., 124n.3

Krueger, Alan, 47n.6, 7

Kulik, Jane, 12n.8, 124-25n.6

Labor market: developments in, 111-12; policy framework to facilitate adjustment of, 121-22; private programs to facilitate adjustment in, 123; segments affected by change in structure of job opportunities, 17-18

Levy, Frank, 125n.12

Lovemen, Gary, 48n.14

Macroeconomic policy: effect on employment opportunities of, 3

Madden, Janice F., 101n.5

Mare, Robert, 10

Medoff, James, 47n.8

Mobility. See Employment mobility; Occupational mobility

Occupational mobility, 75, 78, 81

Occupations: change for displaced workers of, 68; change in distribution and structure of opportunities for, 27, 111; comparable-wage for displaced workers, 75-77; differences in composition of declining-sector and growth-sector, 113; increase in service-producing, 24; shift toward better-educated and trained workers, 21, 23; See also Employment opportunities

Podgursky, Michael, 47n.10, 101n.4, 101n.10

Preferences for reemployment, 70

Public policy: to facilitate programs for labor market adjustment, 121-23; present and future focus of, 8-9, 18-20; proposed focus, 112, 120-121; response to job displacement problems, 2-8; theoretical basis for, 29-30

Reemployment: in comparable-wage sector, 114; of displaced workers, 7, 30-32, 66-70, 79, 111; earnings of displaced workers in, 30-32, 112; likelihood of, 18; opportunities in service sector for, 24-25

Regional adjustment: in employment opportunities, 42-46

Rents, economic: loss by displaced workers of, 112-13

Retraining. See Job training; for displaced worker seeking employment, 62

Ruhm, Christopher, 47n.10, 101n.5

Seitchik, Adam, 47n.9, 125n.11

Service-producing sector: growth in limited-skill jobs in, 24-25; increase in jobs in, 3

States' role in EDWAA, 8

Summers, Lawrence, 47n.6, 47n.7, 124n.1

Swaim, Paul, 47n.10, 101n.4, 101n.10

Tilly, Chris, 48n.14

Training programs: for displaced workers, 121; under EDWAA, 9; effectiveness of, 7; See also Economic Dislocation and Worker Adjustment Assistance Act (EDWAA); Job Training Partnership Act (JTPA)

Transition programs, federal: for displaced workers, 3-4

Transition programs, private: for education and training, 4; to facilitate displaced worker adjustment, 123-24

Unemployed workers, long-term: compared to workers in growth and nongrowth sectors, 25-27, 29; skill mismatches for growth industry jobs, 28-29; See also Workers, semiskilled

Unemployment: increase for specific groups in, 18-19; rates and duration of, 13-15; reasons for, 15

United States Departments of Labor and Treasury, 125n.13

United States General Accounting Office, 12n.6, 125n.10

Voucher system under EDWAA, 7-8
Vroman, Wayne, 125n.13

Wage and salary quartiles: changes in
 composition of employment in, 39-42
Wage opportunities: adjustment on
 regional level, 45-46; changing
 structure of, 29, 39-42
Wages: displaced workers with high,
 16-17; displaced workers with low,
 114-15
White-collar employment: shift of blue-
 collar to, 111; shift of opportunities
 toward, 21
Winship, Christopher, 10
Worker Adjustment and Retraining
 Notification Act (WARN), 11n.1
Workers: characteristics of growth-sector,
 61; earnings pattern for full-time, 27;
 effect of economic development on, 2;
 groups represented among unemployed,
18-19; systems for allocation of, 1-2
Workers, displaced: adjustment to
 economic change, 114; blue-collar,
 skilled and semiskilled, 75, 79;
 characteristics of, 61, 70, 72;
 comparable-wage jobs for, 75-77;
 earnings loss for, 7-8, 20-30; high-
 wage, 79, 81, 114; human capital
 attributes of, 70; in low-wage jobs,
 114-15; private programs to facilitate
 adjustment, 123-24; recovery routes for,
 62-64; reemployment of, 7, 30-31,
 66-70, 79, 111; transferability of human
 capital for, 78; *See also* Economic
 Dislocation and Worker Adjustment
 Assistance Act (EDWAA); Job
 Training Partnership Act (JTPA)
Workers, semiskilled: among long-term
 unemployed, 26-27; decline in
 employment among, 24; replacement
 of, 27

129